ARTHUR
NEGUS
Enjoys
COUNTRY · HOUSES

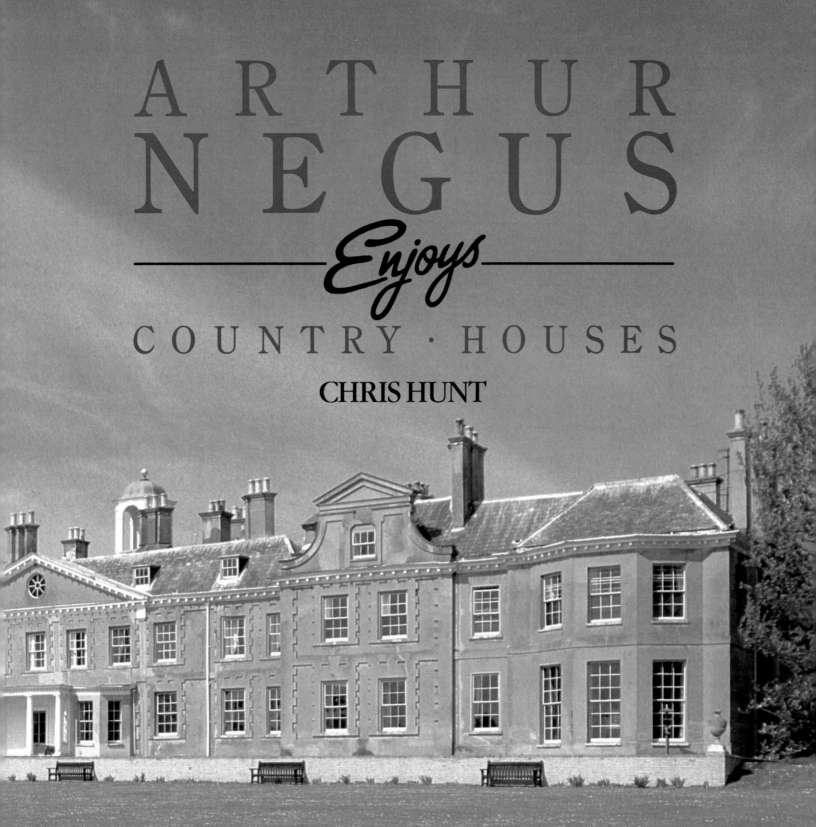

ARTHUR NEGUS
Enjoys
COUNTRY · HOUSES

CHRIS HUNT

BRITISH BROADCASTING CORPORATION/OCTOPUS BOOKS

Endpapers *A detail showing the hand-painted birds and branches of the exquisite Chinese wallpaper in the Drawing Room at Littlecote*
Page 1 *Elaborate marquetry on the front of one of the magnificent 'Panshanger Cabinets' in the upper Drawing Room at Firle Place*
Previous page *The graceful and imposing façade of Stratfield Saye, home of the Duke of Wellington*
Right *The Upper Cloisters at Wilton House*

Acknowledgements

My thanks are due to Robin Drake, executive producer of the BBC television series *Arthur Negus Enjoys*, and the other regular members of the production team – Geraldine Manning, David Mitchell and Theophila Vertis – for their help in the writing of this book. BBC Publications and Octopus Books wish to thank John Bly for his great help in editing it.

Photographs by Adam Woolfitt

Photograph of Arthur Negus by Radio Times

First published in 1985 by The British Broadcasting Corporation
35 Marylebone Street, London W1M 4AA
and Octopus Books Limited
59 Grosvenor Street, London W1X 9DA

© Text: Chris Hunt 1985

© Foreword: Arthur Negus 1985

© Illustrations BBC/Octopus Books Limited

ISBN 0 7064 2310 0 (Octopus)

ISBN 0 563 20250 5 (British Broadcasting Corporation)

Printed in Spain

CONTENTS

Foreword	7
LITTLECOTE	8
WESTON PARK	20
SYON HOUSE	34
WILTON HOUSE	48
FIRLE PLACE	60
GOODWOOD HOUSE	70
TEMPLE NEWSAM HOUSE	82
LUTON HOO	94
KINGSTONE LISLE PARK	108
SHUGBOROUGH HALL	120
DUDMASTON	134
STRATFIELD SAYE HOUSE	146
Index	158

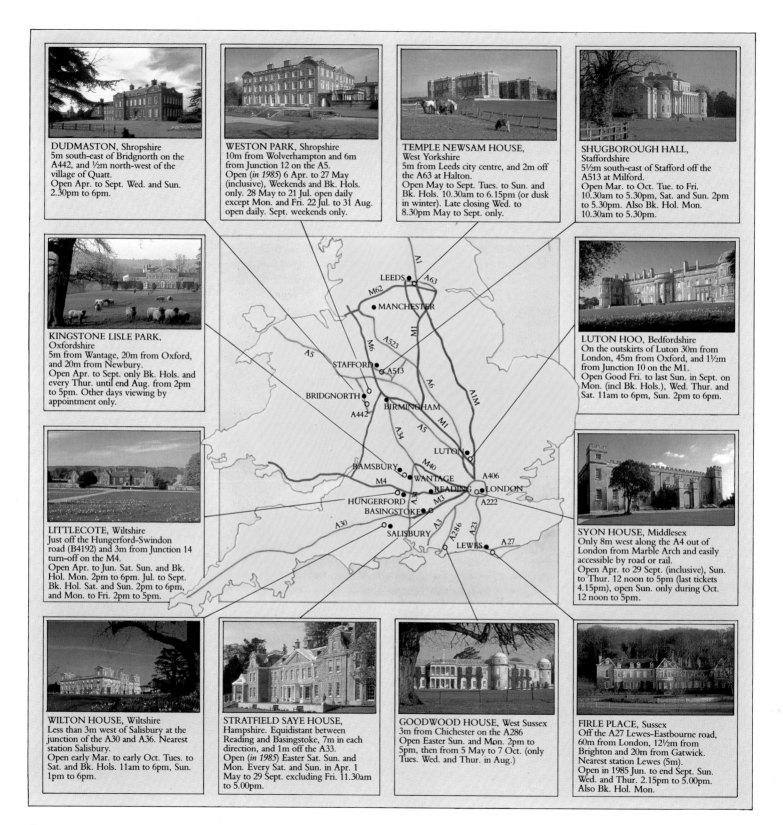

DUDMASTON, Shropshire
5m south-east of Bridgnorth on the A442, and ½m north-west of the village of Quatt.
Open Apr. to Sept. Wed. and Sun. 2.30pm to 6pm.

WESTON PARK, Shropshire
10m from Wolverhampton and 6m from Junction 12 on the A5.
Open (in 1985) 6 Apr. to 27 May (inclusive), Weekends and Bk. Hols. only. 28 May to 21 Jul. open daily except Mon. and Fri. 22 Jul. to 31 Aug. open daily. Sept. weekends only.

TEMPLE NEWSAM HOUSE, West Yorkshire
5m from Leeds city centre, and 2m off the A63 at Halton.
Open May to Sept. Tues. to Sun. and Bk. Hols. 10.30am to 6.15pm (or dusk in winter). Late closing Wed. to 8.30pm May to Sept. only.

SHUGBOROUGH HALL, Staffordshire
5½m south-east of Stafford off the A513 at Milford.
Open Mar. to Oct. Tue. to Fri. 10.30am to 5.30pm, Sat. and Sun. 2pm to 5.30pm. Also Bk. Hol. Mon. 10.30am to 5.30pm.

KINGSTONE LISLE PARK, Oxfordshire
5m from Wantage, 20m from Oxford, and 20m from Newbury.
Open Apr. to Sept. only Bk. Hols. and every Thur. until end Aug. from 2pm to 5pm. Other days viewing by appointment only.

LUTON HOO, Bedfordshire
On the outskirts of Luton 30m from London, 45m from Oxford, and 1½m from Junction 10 on the M1.
Open Good Fri. to last Sun. in Sept. on Mon. (incl Bk. Hols.), Wed. Thur. and Sat. 11am to 6pm, Sun. 2pm to 6pm.

LITTLECOTE, Wiltshire
Just off the Hungerford-Swindon road (B4192) and 3m from Junction 14 turn-off on the M4.
Open Apr. to Jun. Sat. Sun. and Bk. Hol. Mon. 2pm to 6pm. Jul. to Sept. Bk. Hol. Sat. and Sun. 2pm to 6pm, and Mon. to Fri. 2pm to 5pm.

SYON HOUSE, Middlesex
Only 8m west along the A4 out of London from Marble Arch and easily accessible by road or rail.
Open Apr. to 29 Sept. (inclusive), Sun. to Thur. 12 noon to 5pm (last tickets 4.15pm), open Sun. only during Oct. 12 noon to 5pm.

WILTON HOUSE, Wiltshire
Less than 3m west of Salisbury at the junction of the A30 and A36. Nearest station Salisbury.
Open early Mar. to early Oct. Tues. to Sat. and Bk. Hols. 11am to 6pm, Sun. 1pm to 6pm.

STRATFIELD SAYE HOUSE, Hampshire. Equidistant between Reading and Basingstoke, 7m in each direction, and 1m off the A33.
Open (in 1985) Easter Sat. Sun. and Mon. Every Sat. and Sun. in Apr. 1 May to 29 Sept. excluding Fri. 11.30am to 5.00pm.

GOODWOOD HOUSE, West Sussex
3m from Chichester on the A286
Open Easter Sun. and Mon. 2pm to 5pm, then from 5 May to 7 Oct. (only Tues. Wed. and Thur. in Aug.)

FIRLE PLACE, Sussex
Off the A27 Lewes-Eastbourne road, 60m from London, 12½m from Brighton and 20m from Gatwick. Nearest station Lewes (5m).
Open in 1985 Jun. to end Sept. Sun. Wed. and Thur. 2.15pm to 5.00pm. Also Bk. Hol. Mon.

FOREWORD

The BBC approached me in 1980 with a view to making a series of programmes in which I would visit a country house in company with a guest, and we would share our pleasure in the items we found there. This became the series *Arthur Negus Enjoys*, and since then I have visited a number of houses with a number of people, many of whom are friends and colleagues from the world of antiques. One of the aims of these programmes was to communicate not only information about the place, but also its atmosphere and character; in fact not all the programmes dealt specifically with the rooms and *objets d'art* in the various country houses. Each chapter of this book forms a record of my visit with my guest to one of these houses, and includes at times more background details than it was possible to give in the programme; while the views and judgments in the book, except where specifically attributed, are those of the author, not me, it is faithful to the content and tone of the television series. I hope it will enable those who watched the programmes, and also those who didn't, to share some of my enjoyment in the houses I visited.

Arthur G. Negus

LITTLECOTE

Littlecote is a Tudor manor-house, dating from the end of the fifteenth century. Lying between Hungerford and Ramsbury, it is the most important brick mansion in Wiltshire and may well be the earliest. Arthur came here with a friend of many years' standing, the well-known expert in ceramics – and particularly Worcester porcelain – Henry Sandon.

They began in one of the most striking rooms in the house, the Great Hall. It is entered through an Elizabethan screen and has, in a roundel in the high window, the initials of King Henry VIII and Jane Seymour – united with lover's knots, and a cupid's head for good measure – for it is said that the king courted Jane from Littlecote. Certainly the marriage took place at her father's house nearby, the day after the beheading of her predecessor, Anne Boleyn.

However, the rest of the Hall bespeaks the middle of the seventeenth century, the time of Oliver Cromwell. Arthur pointed out the oak all around – in the table, in big, bold chairs, in the panelling on all the walls. And above the panelling, there is an extraordinary collection of arms and armour. It formed part of the arsenal of the private army maintained by the man who owned the house at the time, Alexander Popham. He it is who sits proudly on horseback in the portrait at the west end of the Hall. The officers and men of his Littlecote Garrison wore buff coats, some of which are displayed on the walls. Henry described them as being reminiscent of buffalo skins, hence the word 'buff'. Also on the walls is a fine display of flintlock pistols, and numerous muskets, all with the monogram 'AP', showing that they were given by Popham himself for his men to use. He fought, surprisingly perhaps, on the side of Parliament against the king in the Civil War. Though an opponent of Charles I, Popham assisted General Monk in restoring Charles II, having apparently become disenchanted with the course of Cromwellian

Right *The South Front. Formal lawns and gardens surround this long, low manor-house. Its striking mellow brick façade is counterpointed by well-established shrubs which climb its walls towards the gabled eaves and Cotswold stone roof*

rule. He obtained the King's Pardon and later, when Charles II was travelling from London to Bath, entertained the king with a great feast in this very Hall. Clearly Popham was fortunate enough to be on the right side at the right time – a useful ability shared, as we shall see, by other owners of major houses.

On the subject of the king, Arthur noted a pewter charger or large dish on the west wall, all of 18 inches in diameter and with a wide flat rim. The whole well of the charger is beautifully engraved, incorporating the royal coat of arms, and featuring above them the Latin text *Vivat Rex Carolus Secondus* – 'Long Live King Charles the Second'. It bears the date 1661; Charles was crowned in 1660. Henry particularly liked the engraved decoration showing the sun rising in splendour over the top, as if the king, like the sun, had returned. And on the rim he noticed an engraved tulip – a contemporary motif also to be found on early pottery. Arthur moved on to the largest object in

the room, by all appearances a ten-legged, 30-foot-long oak refectory table. The table-top is 3 to 4 inches thick, with ten bulbous supports united by square stretchers. In fact it is a games table. You knock ten discs down its length, just as in shove-halfpenny, and there are lines marked near the end to show where to aim for. Appropriately, it is called a shovelboard table. The brass discs fascinated Arthur. His bore the initials 'AA', and Henry picked up one inscribed 'PP'. So when the game was over, you could tell which disc was whose, and hence who had won. Henry observed that this game would have been played here in about 1660. Arthur, who had been busy practising, looked up to point out that he wasn't quite that old!

On the table were a pair of jugs that were of great interest to Henry – two of the finest salt-glazed bellarmine jugs from Germany that he had ever seen. These jugs, dated 1594, are contemporary with the Hall and marked

Left *The Great Hall, looking through the arch of the Elizabethan screen. The big oak shovelboard table dominates the room; behind, on the west wall, the painting of Alexander Popham on horseback is surrounded by the arms and uniforms of his Littlecote Garrison*

Right *A German bellarmine jug, made of salt-glazed stoneware, and used for pouring beer. Part of the coat of arms of Queen Elizabeth I can be made out on the front; dating as it does from the latter period of her reign, the jug is in excellent condition*

with the coat of arms of Elizabeth I. They feature curious caricatures of the exceedingly unpopular Cardinal Bellarmine on the neck. The Italian theologian's lectures were an attempt to combat the Protestant position – so he would hardly have been loved by a Lutheran German public. Such jugs were imported from Germany to rich English houses and used for pouring beer. Henry described their method of production: salt was thrown into the kiln at the highest point of the firing, whereupon it volatilised on the jug surface, giving it a browny, mottled effect, like the skin of an orange. Hence the term 'salt-glazed stoneware'. Arthur admired their condition, pointing out that in a few years' time they would be 400 years old – yet they look robust and solid.

Chinese porcelain was also imported, at enormous expense, to the very wealthy homes of the time. Because of the cost, the English attempted to imitate it, using tin-glazed earthenware. As Henry noted, its white tin glaze covered up a multitude of sins to make it resemble Chinese blue-and-white. To illustrate the difference, Henry first picked up a piece of English delftware off the table. It was a 'posset pot', for serving the drink posset – in Henry's words 'a fiendishly nasty drink of curdled milk and warmed wine. I don't know what it tastes like – I've never dared drink it!' You sucked it from the spout of what looks like a teapot; the one Henry was holding in his hand was decorated with 'charming but naive imitations of Chinese blue-and-white paintings, with silly little

non-Chinese Chinamen doing all sorts of crazy things!'

To emphasise the contrast, Henry picked up a Chinese porcelain dish from the late Ming Dynasty, dating from around 1630, sixty years earlier than the English imitation. Beautiful as it is, it was not just an ornament – it was meant to be used for fruit or other food. As Arthur pointed out, many people may not realise that such pieces were once actually used, because today they are usually seen in cabinets or on walls, for display only. According to Henry, their beauty lies partly in their whiteness but also, in the case of this dish, in its magnificent painting in underglaze cobalt oxide. It would have cost a king's ransom when it came into the country in about 1670 and, apart from being beautiful, it has the quality of ringing like a bell when you strike it. So Henry struck it, and it did. Then he picked up another English piece, a delft blue-and-white plate, and it gave out 'an awful clunk'. There was no comparison at all between the quality of this plate and the previous dish. This one was decorated with tulips, as was the Charles II charger, but dates from around 1690-1700, thirty or forty years later. The decoration is in the Dutch style, as Henry pointed out, in imitation of original Delft. It also features blue dashes all round the rim, hence this kind of plate is known as a 'blue dash charger'.

Moving along the big table, Arthur next came upon a number of flagons. The first he picked up, with a cover shaped like a bun, dates from 1610. As Arthur commented, it is rare to find one as old as this. Alongside it was a pair that are twenty to thirty years younger, strong and Cromwellian. They have flat tops, thumb-pieces shaped like buds, and skirt bases – as Henry interjected, plain but sturdy. Next to these was a leather one. Arthur noted that Cromwellian chairs were often covered in leather, to make them sturdier, and leather was also much used for drinking vessels, which are known as blackjacks. They are even better, as Arthur pointed out, when they have a silver mount, as this one has. The silversmith engraved the figures '2 6½' in the silver, denoting that there are 2 ounces, 6½ pennyweights of silver in the mount. The blackjack's big brother was standing next to it. According to Arthur, it would hold three to four gallons of ale; it is big, plain, strong as it looks, and called a bombard.

After all that drink, Arthur suggested that a seventeenth-century man would need to sit down and rest so, moving to the fire-place, he began to consider the chairs in the room. The first he looked at is a big Elizabethan one, dating from around 1600 and known as a turnery chair because all the wood would have been turned on a primitive pole-lathe. There is a great deal of wood in it – ash and oak – and as Arthur said, it is marvellous how they did so much turning to produce one chair; but it still looks very uncomfortable to sit in.

It is, in fact, contemporary with the portrait of Sir John Popham that hangs near it. He was the first of the Popham family to own Littlecote, coming into possession in 1589 when the previous owner, William 'Wild' Darrell, was killed while hunting in the park. The official story is that it was an accident, but many suspect that he was murdered by men in the service of his neighbour Sir Walter Hungerford. At all events, he seems to have earned his nickname. Apart from many accusations of unlawful land seizure and appalling debts, he was implicated in more than one murder. He also probably carried on a passionate affair with Lady Ann Hungerford, which her husband almost certainly knew about. And Popham, Darrell's cousin, spent much of his time as a lawyer keeping Darrell out of jail. The price for his agreeing to do so may have been Littlecote itself.

Though the present building dates from the early Tudor period, there was a house slightly to the west of the present one from about 1200. The de Calston family owned it then but it passed to the Darrell family by

marriage in 1415. They owned Littlecote until Sir John Popham came along, and the Pophams owned it until 1922, when it was acquired by Sir Ernest Salter Wills. He was largely responsible for the present excellent condition of the house; his grandson now owns it and lives in it.

John Popham improved the house once he became owner, and the south façade, for instance, is his work. He was also responsible for the building of the Great Hall in 1590 – Henry speculated that he may have bought the turnery chair for his new room. When not altering Littlecote, Sir John found time to be Lord Chief Justice of England, a post which saw him presiding over the trials of Sir Walter Raleigh and Guy Fawkes. Next to the chair is a small reminder of his position: a finger stock, supposedly used by him to confine prisoners in the dock.

Arthur then turned to a French-style chair known as a caquetoire. It dates from about 1620, making it roughly contemporary with the turnery chair. In France at this time chairs were always made in walnut. It is also known that a few such chairs were copied in England in the first quarter of the seventeenth century in oak – but this one is neither oak nor walnut. As Arthur recounted, its story is known because it bears the arms of a merchantman called Richard Roope, who sent a ship to Brazil in 1617 which returned with '175 ends of red and speckled wood'. This chair is made of such wood – mahogany – and is remarkable because mahogany for furniture only came in any quantity to England around 1730, a whole century later. So this could be one of the earliest known mahogany chairs of English manufacture in England today.

Arthur noted that the caquetoire looks very solid and strong, with straight arms. As English chairs developed during the seventeenth century the arms tended to drop forward and become more graceful. The legs were then often turned, the under-supports became finer and more detailed, and the whole chair began to look more attractive. Arthur pointed to the inlaid chair by the fire-place as a good example. As he noted, inlay began to be used, usually in holly or box, with bog oak for the black elements, and occasionally sycamore – all native woods. The chair developed a cresting-rail joining the upright across the chair-back, and brackets on the sides. All these features help to date a seventeenth-century chair.

Arthur then turned to a chair from the last quarter of the same century and here the primary feature is carving. The

Left *More accessories for the beer-swilling Cromwellian. On the left, a pewter flagon; on the right, its leather equivalent, a blackjack. This one is the more prized for its silver mounts. Behind them (centre), a challenge for even the most serious drinker; a bombard, holding three or four gallons*

Above *Two seventeenth-century chairs by the Great Hall fire-place. The chair on the right has graceful arms, and a great deal more carving – including the date 1679 on the cresting-rail – than the caquetoire on the left from half a century later*
Left *The Elizabethan turnery chair in the Great Hall: a great deal of wood, but not much comfort*

Right *This picture of Littlecote in 1660, painted by Thomas Wycke, hangs over the Great Hall fire-place. The building itself seems to have changed little in the intervening three centuries, though the grounds have*

back, the tops of the arms, the panel, the cresting-rail and the brackets are all covered with carving, including the initials of a former owner, and a date: 1679. Many dates on furniture are, as Arthur warned, phoney, but this one is quite genuine. So these chairs by the fire-place form an instructive contrast in seventeenth-century styles, though all are solid, straight-backed and strong. Above the fire-place is a picture that Henry particularly liked, showing the exterior of Littlecote in 1660, very much as it is today.

Arthur and Henry then jumped forward a century by entering the Drawing Room and the contrast was obvious and immediate. The first sensation that Arthur noted distinguishing the Drawing Room from the Hall was that of colour. Gone are the sombre flagstones and drab walls, to be replaced with beautiful carpets and wallpaper, while graceful shapes and delicate furniture contrast greatly with the strong, stiff oak pieces in the Hall.

The walls, for example, are hung with exquisite Chinese wallpaper, hand-painted with branches and birds. Arthur remembered that when he was a young man he could never understand how it was that rooms of Chinese wallpaper were able to be sold. He had no idea then that it was mounted on linen so that it could be transported. To demonstrate, he touched the wallpaper, showing that it was loose on the wall.

Henry then observed that the porcelain of the eighteenth century is also delicate and colourful. He looked first at a pair of Worcester vases dating from around 1790, with pink-scaled grounds and gorgeous gilding. In the panels are exquisite Chinese-style painted figures. By now the Worcester imitation Chinamen had become well enough established for them to be called Worcester figures. Henry described them as 'Gilbert and Sullivan Chinese'. They are beautiful and very rare vases.

Near them on another table, though usually on view in the Long Gallery, were 'some of the most magnificent Worcester pieces I've ever seen in my life'. Coming from Henry Sandon, one of the world's leading experts on the subject, that is praise indeed. They are a garniture or set of pot-pourri vases for putting dried, sweet-smelling flowers into and they are encrusted all over with hand-made, stuck-on flowers and ribbons. There are also butterflies and other insects in the decoration, and holes carved out to create frills. As Henry explained, the man who built up

such an item would have been called a 'repairer' – quite a different use of the term. Repairers usually put their own marks on the base and, sure enough, on these Henry found the initials 'TO', which stands for John Toulouse, who was at Bristol and Chelsea before moving to Worcester in about 1770. Henry's verdict: 'quite the most scrumptious thing imaginable'.

The vases stood on what Arthur in reply called a 'snorter' of a table. It is an oval Pembroke table in mahogany. As he noted, these are pieces on which a cabinet-maker would often show off. This one has a drawer that carries the same curved shape as the top, which is cross-banded with satinwood; the square taper legs are beautifully inlaid with bluebell drops.

There are, in fact, a pair of these tables, though they are normally on view in the Library rather than the Drawing Room. On the second table of the pair Henry found two superb plates. The first is from a Worcester service made for the Duke of Gloucester in about 1770, and decorated with very colourful fruit – with spots. The painter's name is not known so he is called the 'spotted fruit painter'. Holding the plate up to the light, Henry observed its green translucence, a delicate hue characteristic of Worcester at that time. In this it differs greatly from the plate next to it, from the Chelsea factory – heavier and less translucent, but decorated with fruit as well. This time one of the fruits is sliced so, sure enough, the painter is known as the 'sliced fruit painter'. On the base of the plate Henry pointed out the red anchor which is the mark of the Chelsea factory. He noted that on genuine pieces the mark is tiny but on

Right *A pair of rare Worcester vases dating from about 1770. The pink-scaled ground surrounds bright and colourful panels featuring delightful Chinese-style figures*

Left *The Drawing Room, which was formed in the mid-eighteenth century, and altered in 1810, when the delightful Chinese wallpaper was introduced. This elegant room with its graceful furniture exemplifies the move away from the sturdy but ponderous furnishing of earlier times*
Below *These bright and graceful birds and branches are hand-painted onto the loose-hanging Chinese wallpaper in the Drawing Room*

fakes it is often much larger, up to about half an inch in size.

The final piece of furniture that Arthur looked at was a splendid George I walnut card-table. The two back legs pull out square, so that there is a leg at each corner, and in the top are guinea wells, for money. There are also wooden roundels at the corners, possibly for placing candlesticks on. In all, as Arthur commented, a table like this is a pleasure to sit at and lose your money.

On this occasion there was some more porcelain on it, including part of an enormous service made at Worcester around 1780, which Henry described as one of Littlecote's greatest treasures. The pieces have blue grounds and painted scenes, all different, from fables by Aesop or Gay. Henry admired one depicting a fox who has fallen in the

17

water, surrounded and attacked by a swarm of bees, while a hedgehog laughs from the bank. Another dish he and Arthur looked at shows a donkey and a dog chatting in an English landscape. The beautifully painted panel has honey gilding around it. As Henry explained, this is gold powdered in honey; it creates a softer and browner effect than the mercuric oxide gilding which came in later, around 1790. The dish also has borders cut out when the clay was wet. The incised marks made by the reticulator who did it, to set out the exact pattern of holes, are still discernible. Also set out on the table were a number of china cows of all descriptions. They are cream jugs, collected at Littlecote from almost every factory in the nineteenth century. It was the final set of pieces Arthur and Henry had time to look at, but there are other rooms and objects worth mentioning, here as at other houses.

The rest of the cream jugs can be seen in the Long Gallery, along with an excellent array of paper weights. Both these collections were built up by the late Lady Wills. The Long Gallery, all 110 feet of it, is a handsome and impressive room with a floor and wall panelling both of oak. Here is a feast of furniture, china and glass of many styles and periods, including several commodes, one of which is Louis XV, and some Chippendale armchairs covered with needlework of a similar design to the fine Queen Anne carpet by the fire-place. A number of large portraits hang here, nearly all of which are of the Popham family.

Adjoining the Drawing Room is a conservatory which was built in 1810; it now contains a heated swimming-pool, installed in 1935. Also built in 1810 was the Library, a semi-elliptical room. Among the volumes it contains are the law books of Lord Chief Justice Popham, whose annotations can be seen. It also features a fine Aubusson carpet, which originally belonged to Queen Charlotte, wife of King George III. The carpet in the Drawing Room is also an Aubusson, but owned this time by Louis XV and used originally in the Palace of Versailles. The library bookcases are oak and the furniture includes some delicate Sheraton satinwood pieces, including a little table painted with peacock's feathers and bouquets of flowers.

Littlecote boasts a number of rooms of an earlier date that merit a mention. The Brick Hall (so called because its floor is brick) was until recently strewn in the traditional way with scented rushes from nearby water-meadows. It

has fine seventeenth-century panelling, behind which is a secret passage for listening to what was being said in the Library. The Cromwellian chapel is believed to be the only complete surviving example of its type. There is no altar, but in its place an elevated pulpit. And the William of Orange Bedroom is so named because he slept at Littlecote in 1688. Above the fire-place is a large tapestry, one of a set of sixteen made for him in the last quarter of the seventeenth century in Brussels. It depicts Apollo and Hercules as supporters of his arms as king of England. Similarly, Queen Elizabeth I's Bedroom has her coat of arms over the fire-place; she stayed here in 1601.

But the room with the most curious story is known as the Haunted Bedroom. Arthur recounted its gruesome past in a television programme some years ago. It seems

Left *One of the garniture of late eighteenth-century Worcester pot-pourri vases. Its flair and intricacy moved Worcester porcelain connoisseur Henry Sandon to heights of praise. A garniture was originally a set of matching ornaments for chimney-piece or mantelpiece*

Right *A Worcester dish, from about 1780, featuring exquisite honey gilding, and a donkey in conversation with a dog. All the pieces in this service feature various scenes from fables by Aesop or Gay. This one depicts Aesop's fable 'The Ass and the Lap-Dog'*

that in 1575 William Darrell sent for a midwife to attend a lady about to have a child. The midwife was blindfolded and not told where she was going – nor did she ever see the face of the woman in labour. Nonetheless, she delivered a boy child, under threat of death should the lady miscarry, but once she showed the baby to the waiting gentleman, he ordered her to throw it into the fire. She was bribed to keep silent about this horrible affair, but her conscience eventually forced her to go to the magistrate and confess all she knew. She identified Littlecote, and evidence was collected by Darrell's neighbours. The midwife's story was discovered among letters written by Darrell from the Fleet Prison, London, in 1579, after giving evidence. This appalling tale features in Sir Walter Scott's poem 'Rokeby'. The Haunted Bedroom is where the child was

born, and the unknown mother also apparently died. But another version claims that the mother was Lady Hungerford and that she did not die there at all, but eventually returned to her home. Either way, this was the worst of many accusations levelled at 'Wild' Darrell and it is also probably the specific charge that forced him to bribe Sir John Popham with Littlecote itself, to use his legal position to get him acquitted.

So Littlecote is a Tudor manor-house steeped in history, some glorious, some ghoulish. Its contrasting rooms, furniture and other objects are fascinating and instructive, offering Arthur and Henry Sandon a fine opportunity to make comparisons between the styles of different centuries, and also to enjoy some unusual furniture and porcelain.

WESTON PARK

Weston Park, near Shifnal, close to the border between Shropshire and Staffordshire, is a house that Arthur Negus has visited many times, and whose State Rooms are very familiar to him. Many of these are exciting and impressive. The Tapestry Room features a set of very rare Gobelins tapestries, and the Library and Drawing Room, both fine rooms in themselves, also boast a number of good paintings, while the Marble Hall leads to a beautiful balustrade and staircase. And there are many other rooms – but on this occasion Arthur's visit was not concerned with them directly. For he had brought with him a specialist from the Victoria and Albert Museum, Madeleine Ginsburg, an expert in period clothing, to talk about the costumes people would have worn, their make-up, and their preparations to make themselves presentable to their visitors, back in the eighteenth century. It is a subject that, as Arthur observed, fascinates many thousands of people, and for the discussion of which Weston Park is, as we shall see later in the chapter, admirably equipped.

Arthur and Madeleine began by looking at a portrait miniature upstairs in one of the bedrooms. Madeleine dated the lady depicted to about 1780, and very pretty she was with her pink cheeks and neat, powdered hair. Madeleine joked that she must have spent almost as much time painting and arranging herself as the miniaturist did in painting her portrait! For the ladies of the time were dressed and made-up extremely elaborately, in accordance with the fashion of the time. The lady in the miniature has a similar appearance to Elizabeth, wife of the 1st Baron Bradford, who is the subject of a full-size picture hanging on the wall. This would have been painted somewhat earlier, around 1755 to 1760, but the features are the same: pink cheeks in a face that looks enamelled and perfect, and white hair. Elizabeth would have been about twenty at the time and her portrait was painted in Paris where it was the

Right *The exterior of Weston Park, viewed from the south-east. The main entrance was moved to the east in the nineteenth century by the 3rd Earl (of the second creation), to whom much of the look of the present house is due*

fashion to powder the hair so that, regardless of its natural colour, it looked white and went with the pale but exquisite face.

Elizabeth Simpson, a Derbyshire heiress, married the young Henry Bridgeman in 1755, seven years before he inherited a house that had been built nearly a century earlier. From his time onwards, Weston Park was to remain the seat of the Bridgeman family, and Henry made several changes to the estate. 'Capability' Brown was brought in to landscape the grounds and the results of his work, including the Temple Pool, can still be seen today. And James Paine, who also worked at Kedleston Hall, Chatsworth, Nostell Priory and other major houses, designed the Roman bridge at one end of the Temple Pool and one quite outstanding garden building: the Temple of Diana. It was built out of stone from the park, and comprises an octagonal room for music, a team room, bedrooms, a dairy and a room intended to be 'the habitation of the dairy woman', not to mention a 'dismal stone bath'. It is reckoned to be one of the finest garden buildings in England, and features beautiful delicate stucco work, along with paintings by the Swiss artist, G. B. I. Columba. Paine also made some improvements to the interior of the house, including a chimney-piece for the Breakfast Room costing £68.6s.8½d., and for the Library (now the Entrance Hall) a 'chimney-piece with antique ornaments on the term and frieze'.

Records exist of the running and feeding of the household then. In 1771 a sheep weighing 50 lb was bought for 16s.8d., along with seventeen chickens at 1s.3d. each. Three ducks were 3s.9d., and in 1779 eggs were a halfpenny each, with salmon a mere fivepence a pound. In one month the household succeeded in downing no less than 3,958 quarts of milk. Even with a huge staff, that's an extraordinary amount. Facts such as these repose in plenty in the muniment rooms at Weston Park, where there are thousands of documents dealing with all the minutiae of life here.

Henry Bridgeman died in 1800, six years after he had been created Baron Bradford. He had been responsible for the purchase of a lot of furniture, much of it French, and perhaps he obtained the piece that Arthur and Madeleine went on to admire in the bedroom. It is a late eighteenth-century chest, with a bold serpentine front, canted (bevelled) corners, shaped ends and a burr yew or

amboyna veneer. It has ormolu handles and is a beautiful object. As Arthur pointed out, not surprisingly it is one of a pair – they never seemed to go in for things in singles! Though the furniture is not always laid out this way, on this occasion the chest was standing underneath the portrait of Elizabeth and on it was a delightful mirror, which she would no doubt have used when dressing and making up. The mirror is part of a toilet service, the rest of which was laid out on an adjacent dressing-table.

Here were a number of silver pots of various shapes and sizes. Arthur picked one up and asked Madeleine what would have been put in them. The one he had chosen was fairly easy to identify. The cap was removed to reveal a number of holes in the top – so the whole thing looked rather like an overgrown salt-cellar. These holes are the clue for, as Madeleine pointed out, it is a perfume sprinkler, which would have been used to shake scent into gloves or muffs, in the days before perfume sprays existed.

Other pots were less specific in function, and Madeleine explained that they would have been used for various powders and pomades (scented ointments for the skin and

Left *The portrait of Elizabeth, Lady Bridgeman, aged twenty. Her hair is powdered and her face enamelled to a flawless but artificial perfection*

Right *A late eighteenth-century chest, veneered in burr yew or amboyna, with mercury gilt handles. On it stands the mirror from Lady Ann Newport's silver toilet service*

Left *Not an overgrown salt-cellar, but a perfume sprinkler, used for shaking scent into gloves or muffs before the days of perfume sprays. This is another item from Lady Ann Newport's toilet service*
Far left *The rest of Lady Ann Newport's toilet service, made in 1679 and still in excellent condition. Each item carries a separate hallmark, even if it functions in combination with other pieces*

hair), for hair grease, perfumes and skin paints. As the portraits showed, ladies used to try to enamel themselves into a mask of perfection. But they used materials that would horrify us today – such as white lead, which has the disadvantage of being poisonous. Its effect is to make the skin spotty and blotchy so they tried to clear it up by using mercury, or even chloride of lime, which is more like a lavatory cleaner than a cosmetic! The price of beauty in those days could be high indeed.

The toilet set is quite remarkable, from the pincushion right up to the mirror. It was made in 1679, towards the end of Charles II's reign, but 300 years later it is still in quite excellent condition. The pots carried corrosive substances in them, as we have seen, but there is no sign of damage to the silver. Instead, Arthur found a number of features that he liked a great deal, including a very clear set of hallmarks. He picked up a circular pot and noted that the lid is marked separately from the base, as it should be. Every separate piece of silver should carry its own mark, even if it functions in combination with other pieces. These marks were made with individual punches, and were placed with little regard to the decoration. On the lid in Arthur's hand the decoration is almost defaced by the hallmarks – there are some beautifully embossed figures and cherubs – but the marks were punched very close to them so that they intrude into the decorative scene. Nowadays, as Arthur explained, they would no doubt discreetly pop the hallmark underneath, out of sight. But here, Madeleine observed, thay have put it in about the most prominent place possible.

The mirror, the principal item in such a toilet service, is set in an embossed silver frame. It is also Caroline and contemporary with the rest of the service. But there are wall-sconces on either side of the frame which seem, as Arthur put it, to have been just poked onto the sides. Their purpose is clear. It was obviously hard for a seventeenth- or eighteenth-century lady to get enough light to make up by, so these wall-sconces, with candlesticks which swing round to illuminate the front of the mirror, solve that problem. They are wonderful examples of their kind, but they were probably just two of a number that the family had and put to use here, for they are dated 1713, more than thirty years later than the mirror.

But what happened if you got too near the fire when you were wearing some of these cosmetic washes? As Madeleine pointed out, you turned yellow! Hopefully that didn't happen with just a candle flame. For not only was white lead used in face powder, but rouges were coloured with vermilion (which has a mercury base) and iron oxide. These substances were also the basis of paints at the time. Even worse, white arsenic in water was used to soften the skin, before chloride of mercury whitened it and chloride of lime cleaned it. Soap? Well, that was a luxury item, as one of the ingredients (alkali) was in short supply. The result of all this was swelling, inflammation, a change in the texture of the skin, destruction of the teeth, and pimples that then had to be covered up with patches.

It was clearly a dangerous matter to make yourself beautiful in those days but, as Arthur went on to observe, it was equally dangerous if you wanted to beautify furniture with, for example, ormolu handles like those on the chest beneath the mirror. Ormolu is bronze that has been coated with gold. The gold is first mixed with mercury to form an amalgam. The mixture is then applied to the bronze article and heated until the mercury evaporates, leaving the gold firmly affixed to the surface of the bronze and ready for burnishing. Unfortunately, the vapours given off were poisonous and many people died as a result of working with this process.

Looking back at the toilet service, Madeleine added that

make-up could also be fatal. The white enamel look may seem strange to us today. It wasn't a naturalistic effect at all but an expression of a fashionable ideal of beauty – but then if you think about it, today's notions of beautifully made-up faces are also more artistic than naturalistic. The difference is that in those days striving for an artistic effect could be the last thing you ever did.

The owner of the toilet service was in fact Lady Elizabeth's mother-in-law, Lady Ann Newport. She was descended from the original owners and builders of Weston Park, Sir Thomas and Lady Wilbraham. The latter seems to have been the dominant partner in getting the house built around 1670, and a portrait of her in a somewhat unlikely pose, pointing at some tulips, hangs in the pillared Drawing Room. Her daughter Mary, whose

Left *The lid of a circular pot from the toilet service, featuring a beautifully embossed scene with figures and cherubs*

Right *A wall-sconce on the side of the Caroline mirror from the silver toilet service. Such sconces would have been attached to the mirror to provide light for a lady to make up by, but the ones at Weston Park are in fact more than thirty years later in date than the mirror*

Above and right *The Dutch wardrobe, dating from 1730-40, in figured walnut. Above, it is seen closed; on the right, with the doors open. The shelves for laying out dresses can clearly be seen, though they may be uncomfortably high to be used by a lady*

portrait can be seen in the Marble Hall, inherited Weston on her mother's death. Mary's husband was Sir Richard Newport, 2nd Earl of Bradford (of the first creation – the line of earls later died out and was eventually re-created). He had once had occasion to teach manners to a band of highwaymen, when travelling between Leominster and Worcester in his coach. One of the band had fired without ordering the coachman to 'stand and deliver', which was apparently a grave breach of etiquette. Richard duly fired back and killed the villain responsible, while the others fled. Mary and Richard must have had much sadness, for five of their sons died during Mary's lifetime and another became an imbecile after a riding accident and lived most of his life in seclusion. But Mary had daughters too, one of whom was Ann Newport who married Orlando Bridgeman, a lawyer of great eminence and wealth. After the Restoration he became Lord Chief Baron of the Exchequer, Lord Chief Justice of the Common Pleas and Lord Keeper of the Great Seal. They settled near Oswestry and had a town house as well, in Soho Square. But in August 1725 it fell down and, according to the *Whitehall Evening Post*, Lady Ann was 'now great with Child, and near her time of lying in. The Lady being in this condition, and in Bed, was carried out backwards by a servant that perceived the House crack on the fore part. . .'. The child was safely delivered the following month, was called Henry and, as we have seen, came to own Weston.

Arthur and Madeleine, meanwhile, had moved on from considering make-up and its attendant dangers to looking at how Henry or his wife Elizabeth might have dressed. First they came to a wardrobe, about 6 feet 6 inches wide and very tall, in nicely figured walnut. Arthur immediately identified it as Dutch, dating from 1730-40, which prompted Madeleine to ask how he could tell its country of origin. The secret is in the drawers, as Arthur demonstrated. He pulled one out, commenting on the quality of finish on its side, and indicated to Madeleine a small strip of veneer right by the joint. It happened that on the other side of the drawer the equivalent strip of veneer was missing. This gave the game away for it exposed a butt joint, which was nailed together. Now, as Arthur explained, it is no criticism of the standard of workmanship but such a drawer could not be English, because the joints would be dovetailed, not nailed. Hard linings and nailed butt joints are the signs of Dutch cabinet-making.

As Madeleine commented, the wardrobe drawers would hold the small items, just as they do today. The dresses, however, would be laid out flat along a number of racks above the drawers. These shelves run the whole width of the wardrobe, so that no folding at all would be required. Dresses, suits, or other large garments would be stacked on the racks. With very little height between the shelves, there would not be much room to lay many clothes on top of each other. Some wardrobes, though not the one they were looking at, even have sliding shelves that can operate as a kind of clothes-press. But what Madeleine found curious was that the top shelves of the wardrobe were very high – too high for her to reach without some kind of ladder – so the wardrobe was certainly high enough to hang clothes in, but it was many, many years before they got round to doing so.

On one of the shelves Arthur found a few clothes-hangers but they were from the late nineteenth century and Madeleine had never heard of hangers from an earlier date. For Victorian dresses you needed a very high wardrobe to cope with the trains. For this reason, Victorian hangers are not shaped precisely like those of today, but have an extra long rod that runs vertically down from the centre of the hanger. This would enable people to pick a dress off the hanging hook or rail without having to reach all the way up to the top of the hanger. Also, the hangers of this age tended to have a rather wide, swan-necked shape, which would even support an off-the-shoulder bodice.

Returning to the eighteenth century, Madeleine found displayed upon a circular table a number of other items which would help a lady get dressed tidily. First there were some pins in a pincushion; this would be hung discreetly below her dress, out of sight but never out of mind. An eighteenth-century lady would use pins as we now use hooks and eyes, to hold her dress together. The pincushion they were looking at bears the embroidered date '1784' – so it might have been used by the lady in the miniature painting.

Next Madeleine discovered a bodkin, with a little rectangular slot cut along its length, for the tapes which kept a lady's petticoat up, and a little round hole at the end, perhaps for her corset laces if they came untied. It would have been kept in a bodkin case and a charming white enamel example was also on the table.

And for basics, Madeleine showed Arthur a horn comb. Its teeth were quite widely spaced, but then they would have to be. Considering the grease and powders that were put into the hair, it would be no easy matter getting through it all. The tangles would be combed out with the teeth, while the hair would be parted using a long, sharp point at one end of the comb. So, as Arthur summed it up, what a rigmarole it was for a lady to dress in those days! But once she had finally done so, however long it took her, and with whatever unrecognised risks to her personal safety, where would she go next?

Madeleine suggested she would now be ready to appear in public, and would perhaps go to her sitting room, or boudoir, which is where Arthur and she now duly moved on to.

The Boudoir at Weston Park is a delightful room, but what first attracted Arthur's fancy was an item that normally lives elsewhere in the house, on the family portrait landing. It is a small bronze of a reclining figure on a sofa, a piece of furniture that might well have been in a lady's boudoir. The sofa is, in fact, Regency – a single scroll-end example, with four shaped ormolu legs – but the reclining lady has, as Arthur put it, a bit of bother coming her way. Madeleine identified an asp on the lady's chest – for she is none other than Cleopatra, and about to end it all.

The bronze is, as Madeleine noted, very much in the classical style, as is a little Wedgwood jasper or fine

stoneware patchbox she was holding. The lid carries a design of classical cupids in a chariot, in white on a blue ground, while the rest of the box is in cut steel. This was, as Madeleine explained, a lady's way of making running repairs. Items like these are often known as 'trifles' today, and many others, not all of which come from Weston Park itself, were displayed for Madeleine and Arthur on a table. But they would mostly have been made locally, either at Birmingham or Bilston, as delightful little gifts, souvenirs and keepsakes. There was for a time a flourishing enamelling area around south Staffordshire, and Birmingham became the national centre for such products. Its Soho factory produced little boxes which sometimes bore the legend 'A Trifle from Soho' – souvenirs from a less Rabelaisian area than that other Soho in London's West End. Bilston and Birmingham products are often very hard to tell apart and, to make matters worse, items from both places are nowadays often wrongly ascribed to Battersea (which also had a famous enamel factory, though it only lasted three years, from 1753 to 1756).

Arthur suggested such items would be delightful things to collect, and to prove the point he picked up an exquisite scent bottle with an ormolu stopper and an enamel body. This is decorated with a brilliant display of flowers on a white ground, so fresh and lively that you could almost smell them. He then picked up an ivory patchbox, a memorial to the lady who owned it. Again, it features beautiful enamel decoration, in coloured strips this time –

it seems to be all the more effective for being on ivory.

Madeleine meanwhile was looking at another enamelled object which seemed too big to be just a patchbox. Arthur identified it as a table snuffbox, and suggested it might usually have resided on a lady's tea-table. Madeleine added that ladies would certainly not have been averse to taking snuff in those days. The picture on the top is particularly appropriate, depicting a lady in her boudoir, taking tea with a number of friends.

Arthur then took from his pocket an item which thankfully no visitor will ever find displayed at Weston Park: a number of false teeth, grouped in twos and threes. They are made of Worcester porcelain and demonstrate that in those days people's teeth did indeed go rotten – we have already noted how their make-up ingredients would tend to bring that about anyway, quite apart from the question of dental hygiene – and that they were self-conscious enough to wear false ones. When Madeleine asked how they were secured in the mouth, Arthur indicated six little barbs sticking out of one set and suggested they may have actually been fixed into the gums. They are exceedingly rough and it cannot have been a hygienic or enjoyable experience, which again shows how much people were prepared to suffer in order to present themselves as fashionably as possible.

And that was about all Arthur and Madeleine had time to discuss. This visit had been more concerned with the way the smart set lived in the eighteenth century, in terms of presenting themselves to their peers, than with the house itself, which happened to be an excellent setting for such a conversation. For Weston Park not only contains many of the items a well-groomed lady would have needed but is also a fine house in itself, laden with history and boasting many fine rooms.

We can perhaps pick up the history of the house where we left it, with Henry, Baron Bradford, who died in 1800. His son, Orlando Bridgeman, was described as 'one of the Prince Regent's set in his younger days', and was the only witness to the prince's marriage to Mrs Fitzherbert. Orlando was duly created earl, becoming the 1st Earl of the second (and present) creation in 1815, and set about refurbishing the house extensively. Though there seems to have been little structural work, new furniture, carpets, wallpaper and curtains were brought in, not to mention 'patent water closets and apparatus' and 'a Water Machine for the Attic'.

Orlando was succeeded in 1825 by George, his eldest son, one of whose acts was to cover Weston Park with stucco; it was removed in 1939. He died in 1865, and his elder son, another Orlando, inherited. His wife, Selina, had the dubious pleasure – once she was a grandmother! – of having Benjamin Disraeli fall in love with her. He gave her an Aubusson carpet, and a yellow parrot which was thought to be male. It amazed everyone by laying

Right *A small Wedgwood jasperware patchbox, with a design featuring classical cupids in a chariot*

Right *The Tapestry Room, one of the rooms that Arthur and Madeleine did not visit. On the wall are a rare set of Gobelins tapestries, originally in one of the bedrooms*

twenty-three eggs in twenty-four days, dying – whether of exhaustion or confusion – on the twenty-fourth day. The stuffed bird and the eggs are still at Weston. Its plumage apparently indicates that it was a cock bird!

Not content with presenting the lady with a carpet and parrot of dubious gender, Disraeli showered her with letters, sometimes at a rate of more than one a day, totalling roughly 1,100.

Her husband, meanwhile, had set about extensive alterations to Weston Park, and much of the look of the present house is due to him. The main entrance, for instance, was removed to the east, and the present carriage entrance was built; the Library then became the Front Hall. (This room was redecorated in 1961 when the frieze beneath the cornice was added, and the capitals on the columns were changed, making it a slightly more ornate, but still airy, pillared room.) Orlando then made a new Library out of what used to be the Dining Room. Apart from the other pictures it houses, this room is notable for displaying a portrait of his ancestor and namesake. Orlando, Keeper of the Great Seal, painted by John Riley, presides over a cup made from the silver of the seal itself, and the bag of the Great Seal now framed as a fire-screen. Lacking a Dining Room, the 3rd Earl formed a new one out of smaller rooms, including some first-floor bedrooms. It was recently redecorated and made more sumptuous and ornate. Orlando also built a billiards room in 1865 which is now the First Salon and houses two Aubusson tapestries on the walls. He added a west wing in 1872 but, again, attempts have been made to stamp out the Victorian look of the rooms. All these modern efforts to alter Orlando's work have been made by Mary, Countess of Bradford, wife of the 6th Earl. Her artistic gifts are quite apparent and her redecorations have strikingly altered the look of the house. In all this work, she has taken an active role, supervising all the stages of designing and painting.

The late Lord Bradford opened the house and grounds of Weston Park permanently in 1964; the visitor can now see a number of very impressive rooms, just as Arthur has on past occasions. This time, with Madeleine Ginsburg, he used the evidence in the bedrooms and Boudoir to discover a fascinating story – how an eighteenth-century lady would have dressed for her public, and to what lengths and risks she would have gone to do so.

SYON HOUSE

Arthur's guest at Syon House was not a fellow antiques expert by profession, but a well-loved and admired lady of the stage and small screen – Hannah Gordon. She accompanied him to one of the masterpieces of the architect Robert Adam whose name appears in other contexts in almost every chapter of this book, so important was he and so broad was his canvas. As Arthur and Hannah passed through the Great Hall, with its pale pink, grey and white colours, and on into the Ante-Room, Arthur commented that Syon, along with Kedleston Hall, Derbyshire, is widely reckoned to be among Adam's finest architectural achievements.

What happened was, as Arthur noted, that Sir Hugh Smithson, soon to be created 1st Duke of Northumberland, inherited through his marriage to the Percy heiress a 200-year-old house on the north bank of the Thames, near Brentford. It had at one time been a monastery. There it was – a great, stark, gaunt building, just waiting to be modernised.

Adam wanted to make a square out of the Ante-Room but as it is 6 feet longer one way than the other he had a problem. His solution was to incorporate twelve columns into the design of the room, moving some of them away from the wall so that the effect was that of a square. The eye is then taken by his impressive gilt Ionic capitals, with beams across the top of them and four lovely gilt figures on top. The result is that the room appears to be square when it is not.

Hannah mentioned that the quality of illusion was important to Robert Adam, who was particularly interested in fooling the eye. Arthur added that Adam had gone for three and a half years on the Grand Tour, and never really got Roman and Greek antiquities out of his mind, hence the room is full of Roman grandeur. Robert Adam was born in Kirkcaldy, Fife, in 1728. His college career at what was later to be called Edinburgh University

Left *Syon House as viewed from the Lime Drive. This square building with towers at each corner, close by the river Thames, is more impressive inside than outside*

35

Above *The extensive use of pure gold leaf in the Ante-Room. The Ionic capitals, the friezes with their anthemion motif and egg-and-tongue mouldings, the panels and the lovely figure atop the capitals – all are finished with gold leaf*

Left *The Ante-Room. The columns standing out from the wall help make this rectangular room appear square. Though the room is over 200 years old, it is so bright and in such excellent condition that it looks brand-new. The scagliola floor is particularly well preserved*

eruption of Vesuvius, he seemed to have been courting calamity.

But in January 1758 he returned to London, eager to find major commissions. In 1759 he travelled to Harewood House, Yorkshire, to secure work designing parts of it. In 1760 he began to make designs for Kedleston Hall, and in 1762, still aged only thirty-four, he was invited to work on Syon House.

As Arthur pointed out, when designing Syon Adam clearly seemed to want to create the effect on the duke and his friends that Rome and Greece had had upon him. The Ante-Room is grand and splendid, and as Hannah commented, exhibits that tremendous theatrical effect which characterises all his work. The twelve Ionic capitals to the columns are covered with pure gold leaf, as are the typical Adam friezes, featuring the anthemion or formalised flower all the way round, along with little egg-and-tongue mouldings, and the round moulded centrepiece on the ceiling. But it surprised Arthur that Adam had not designed a floor to match the ceiling, as doing so was one of his great trademarks.

Hannah noted that the floor is made of scagliola, which she described as looking like a kind of eighteenth-century Formica. Scagliola is a material that has been used since Roman times to imitate marble, and was used here in a kind of mosaic. It is made of pulverised selenite, which is applied to a wet ground of gesso, fixed by heat and then highly polished. As Arthur pointed out, this room may be 200 years old but everything, including the floor, looks brand-new. Its remarkable state of preservation must be largely due to the high quality of materials insisted upon by Adam. Even though some of its columns were brought from the bed of the river Tiber, this room is in outstanding condition.

Adam had visions of everything being in harmony, even the fire grate. It is modest and ordinary, according to Arthur, with a serpentine front pierced with anthemia just like the frieze above. Hannah added that Robert Adam could seemingly do it all – architecture, floors, furniture and much besides – and had craftsmen coming from many countries to work for him. That may not seem so remarkable to modern minds, but of course travel was nothing like so easy in those days.

Hannah and Arthur now entered the earliest room that Adam designed at Syon, the Dining Room. It is totally

was interrupted by the 1745 rebellion and the following year he joined his father, the architect William Adam, as an apprentice-assistant. William died in 1748, and two years later Robert and his younger brother James, now in partnership, won their first major commission at Hopetoun House, near Edinburgh.

In October 1754, at the age of twenty-six, Robert set off on his Grand Tour, in the entourage of the younger brother of the Earl of Hopetoun, Charles Hope. Once he got to Rome he was smitten, and spent the first few weeks there apparently doing little but walking about, standing and staring. He had no time to eat or sleep – so he said – because there was so much to see. Rome was glorious, and the Pantheon the most glorious building of them all. Adam stayed there some time, and in 1757 travelled to Dalmatia to look at Diocletian's Palace. This was the inspiration for his Adelphi buildings in London. It was also nearly the scene of a disaster for him. For while he was busy drawing the massive columns in the main courtyard of the palace, he was arrested as a spy. But the commander of the garrison happened by chance to be a fellow Scot and, thanks to him, Adam was released. Having passed en route through Pompeii and narrowly missed a new

Right *One of the big Adam mirrors in the Dining Room, reflecting antique-style figures in the niches opposite, along with two four-light candelabra on their amboyna pedestals*

Left *The Dining Room: gold features again, but this time the room is lighter and more airy in atmosphere. Antique-style Roman figures fill the recesses Adam cut into the walls, which are plain stucco; at either end of this long room there are delightful semicircular apses*

food smells would not linger in any drapes or tapestries.

But it is a long room – 66 feet – with windows only down one side, so how was it lit? Arthur showed Hannah one of the four eight-light candelabra. It sits on a tall pedestal of the pretty wood amboyna and, like all the objects here, is beautifully decorated in the neoclassical style. There are also a couple of four-light candelabra, making a total of forty candles in all. That was all the lighting there would have been. Hannah pointed out the mirrors, noting that they would help increase the level of light.

Then, on a table, Hannah saw another glass chandelier. She recalled that when she was a young girl her grandfather's house in Edinburgh had not only Adam-style fire-places, but also two rather less grand chandeliers. Still, when you walked across the room you could hear the glass tinkle! Arthur added that because of the refraction of light from the glass, these chandeliers are very pretty when they are lit, with the light dancing all about. The one on the table was quite rare, being one of a pair made in Ireland around 1800, and faceted so that it sparkles brilliantly. As Hannah observed, although the Dining Room contains few colours and is predominantly pale pink and gold, the glass still shines like a rainbow and shows blues and greens.

Arthur then turned towards the fire-place which, as he explained, may look very large to modern eyes but was the only form of heating they had. Hannah had heard that they used to get through 96 tons of coal here in the winter months. Even so, as Arthur observed, the unlucky diners who had to sit at the far end of the room by the columns would not have felt much benefit from the fire. None the less it is a beautiful marble fire-place, with characteristic Adam swags, grapes and vine leaves.

Hannah pointed out that everything in the room was designed to harmonise with everything else, even down to the chairs. Arthur was not sure how many chairs there would have been in the set but walking round he counted fourteen, and speculated that there could be another ten or twenty elsewhere. Though designed by Adam, they show French influence, with pretty upholstery in a delicate pink, and pure gold leaf on the carved wood frames.

Walking along the line of chairs, Arthur reached the corner of the room and an object he had been itching to get to. It is a clock by Vulliamy, who worked in the late

different in terms of colour and tone from the Ante-Room, but still very much of a piece with it. Hannah found it her favourite room in the house, because of its light, airy quality. It shows a return to very pale pink, but not the cool, imposing colour combination of the Great Hall; the tone is warmer and enhanced with gold. Arthur was impressed with the Corinthian columns, carved capitals and semicircular apses and found the room absolutely beautiful. Where there would have been gaunt walls in the Elizabethan house, Adam carved big niches and had antique-style Roman figures made to fill the recesses. Hannah identified a feeling of brightness and enjoyment in the room. Perhaps it successfully achieves Adam's declared aim to 'parade the conveniences and the social pleasures of life'. And she noticed that the walls are all of plain stucco. Adam made them this way so that

eighteenth and early nineteenth centuries, and it is signed on the plinth 'Vulliamy, London'. It dates from around 1785, and features a biscuit porcelain figure with a celestial globe leaning over the movement, which is housed inside an ormolu case. The globe actually revolves and, all in all, it is a magnificent clock. But what is even more remarkable about it is the pedestal, over 4 feet high, on which it stands. This is overlaid with scagliola, the material used in the Ante-Room floor, and painted in the centre with an oval panel depicting Apollo driving the chariot of the sun, taken from a design by the Italian, Cipriani. Inside is, of all things, a twelve-pipe organ which plays a selection of tunes. To prove it, Arthur wound it up and it started to play as he and Hannah left the Dining Room to enter the Red Drawing Room.

This room is radically different in tone again. It was originally intended by Robert Adam to be the ante-room to the ladies' proper Withdrawing Room, the Gallery. The idea was to separate the Dining Room from the ladies' Withdrawing Room so that they wouldn't be disturbed by the sounds of revelry which could be expected to issue from the Dining Room!

After the lightness of the other room, colour is again the key here. The ceiling is smothered with coloured roundels, the carpet is bright and colourful, and the walls are hung with plum-coloured Spitalfields silk. The Spitalfields silk factories began in London in the late seventeenth century and a number of Huguenot weavers provided extra stimulus to the industry by their arrival in exile from France in 1685. By the early eighteenth century a wide variety of materials was being produced, including velvets, damasks and figured silk brocades often with gold and silver thread. But the English silk factories always suffered from a shortage of good designers. Most of the patterns were either influenced by or directly copied from French silks. As a result, it is often difficult to distinguish with certainty between silks woven at Spitalfields and those made either at the smaller English factories or on the Continent. But those in the Red Drawing Room are known to be Spitalfields, with a grey pattern of flowers and ribbons shimmering like silver on the plum ground. These wall fabrics were restored in 1965 by Lady Meade-Fetherstonhaugh and her assistants at Uppark, using soap made from a plant called saponaria, which was grown on her estate.

Hannah remarked that the carpet was also in fine condition. It was executed by the well-known English manufacturer Thomas Moore, who had a factory in Moorfields Street, specialising in very high quality products. Some were said to have been modelled on Persian patterns, but all the existing carpets known to be by him were made to designs by Adam. This one is no exception, echoing in its pattern a number of favourite Adam motifs that occur elsewhere in the room. Arthur identified among others honeysuckle, the Grecian key pattern border, swags, laurel and the characteristic big medallion. This carpet is one of the finest of its kind in existence, with a woven signature and the date '1769' at one end, and colours still so pure and brilliant that they look as if the carpet was made yesterday.

Arthur also showed Hannah the Adam fire-place, made

Left *The clock by Vulliamy of London, dating from 1785. The biscuit porcelain figure with its celestial globe leans over the movement; underneath is the 4-foot-high pedestal overlaid with scagliola, which conceals the twelve-pipe organ*

Right *The Red Drawing Room. The walls are hung with Spitalfields silk, and there are over 200 brightly painted roundels in the ceiling, with gilded intersecting hands. Even the carpet is to an Adam design and was made specially for the room*

Above *A detail of the ceiling, showing the extraordinary wealth of decoration*

Left *The fireplace in the Red Drawing Room. The white marble chimney-piece beautifully sets off the applied ormolu work of the Birmingham master-craftsman Matthew Boulton*

by the famous Birmingham silversmith Matthew Boulton. As Arthur explained, Boulton was the finest copier of the great French ormolu-makers, and this is an excellent example of his work. The dentil cornice along the marble fire-place is particularly impressive, with each tooth in gilded bronze. The frieze repeats the Adam motifs of honeysuckle all the way along, with medallions, swags of laurel and lover's knots as in the carpet.

The ceiling is perhaps the most remarkable feature of all. It displays a huge number of roundels set in octagons, painted by Cipriani. To Hannah's disappointment, all these roundels, which are only 15 inches in diameter and many of which contain painted figures, were painted on paper and applied afterwards. She had visions of the artist spending a very long time up a ladder! But Cipriani cannot have done too badly out of it. A letter survives at Syon from him to the Duke of Northumberland in which the artist agrees to paint the whole room at two guineas a piece. With well over 200 roundels in the ceiling, that adds up to quite a price.

Looking now at the furniture in the room, Arthur was eager to show Hannah a little dressing-stool, 'right up a lady's street'. This is an extremely rare example, for it is more than it appears. It opens, the top folds back to make two steps up from the ground, and there are four steps concealed inside. It is a remarkable set of library steps hidden in a dressing-stool – and Hannah was delighted by it.

But if that was a piece to please Hannah the next was one for Arthur. It is a roll-top desk, and it shows just what a good cabinet-maker can do with wood. He showed Hannah the semicircular end first, inlaid with round medallions, oval patera, and a typical Adam urn in a central ebony roundel. The segments are all in burr yew, with the lighter sections in satinwood. It is known as a 'free-standing' piece of furniture, clearly not intended to be placed against a wall as the back is inlaid as well as the front. Arthur explained that it is properly called a 'tambour-top writing-table'. The tambour is the roll-top, made of ½-inch strips of wood, not joined together but stuck down onto strong linen. As the top is pushed back, the strips are flexible enough to tuck themselves under the top. And as Arthur demonstrated it, the pretty interior was revealed. Along the bottom there are little drawers veneered in sycamore and a central door with an oval picture of a lady inlaid in different coloured woods. There is even wooden drapery hanging down like curtains over the pigeon-holes, which Hannah said reminded her of theatre boxes. Finally, the front of the desk is also inlaid with medallions, drapery, swags, and an urn in the centre just for good measure: an ornate and exquisite piece.

Arthur then went over to what he identified as the most photographed piece of furniture of all at Syon: an inlaid chest of drawers designed by Adam. Normally it can be seen in the Long Gallery. According to Arthur it is a bit lively in its inlay, with many of the by now familiar motifs – round medallions, anthemia or honeysuckle, drapery and swags – but it is a little special, for it was made for this house in Chippendale's workshops. Apart from being a magnificent object in its own right, it again reminded Hannah of the marvellous sense of integral harmony in the room, with themes echoed in the carpet, the walls, the fire-place and the furniture.

Another feature that appealed to Hannah was the series of portraits around the walls, not only for their value as paintings – though with artists such as Van Dyck and Sir Peter Lely represented they are impressive enough – but as a tremendous source of reference for anyone in the theatre.

Right *The roll-top desk in the Red Drawing Room. As you can see, it is delightfully inlaid throughout, using burr yew, satinwood and ebony. The motifs are typical of Adam and include medallions, urns, drapery, swags and roundels*

Left *The set of library steps that was in the Red Drawing Room when Arthur and Hannah saw it. It looks delightful, but has a secret to hide . . . because below is the same object. When closed up it reveals that it was something else all along: a pretty little dressing-stool*

All are Stuart portraits and tell a great deal about period hairstyles, about how people posed, and of course how they wore their clothes. Hannah stopped at a portrait by Mignard of Henrietta, Duchess of Orleans to point out the magnificence of her dress. There is plenty of information for any costume designer, for the dress has panels encrusted with jewels and precious stones which must have been of considerable weight. It can hardly have been worn for comfort and Hannah suspected that such a dress would only have been worn for a state occasion.

Next to this is a portrait of Charles I by Sir Peter Lely. It fascinated Hannah because of an uncanny likeness between the look and expression of the king, and the way Sir Alec Guinness played the part of Charles I in the film *Cromwell.* If there was no conscious modelling of one on the other then the coincidental similarity is remarkable.

While Charles I looks stern and impassive, next to him is a picture of King Charles II with Catherine of Braganza, by Jacob Huysmans. As Hannah commented, Charles II had a bit more fun than his father, as various stories in Samuel Pepys's diaries testify. Here he is painted with his wife but he was not short of mistresses, including the Duchess of Portsmouth and, of course, Nell Gwynne. Goodwood House, the subject of another chapter in this book, was given by Charles II to the Duke of Richmond, his son by the Duchess of Portsmouth.

When she was at drama school, Hannah wrote a thesis on the introduction of actresses into the theatre in the eighteenth century. While researching this topic, she looked further back and happened upon an account in Pepys that draws a good contrast between the popularity of the Duchess and Nell Gwynne. For a start, the Duchess of Portsmouth was disliked by the public, who took a great interest in royal affairs, because she was a Catholic. Nell Gwynne, on the other hand, was the people's favourite. She happened to be on her way to the palace one day, when the mob mistook her for the Duchess. They turned nasty, rocking the coach and throwing things and, not surprisingly, Nell became scared; but she managed to be good-natured as usual, and leaned out of the window to say, 'Pray, good people, be civil – I am the *Protestant* whore!'

And with that story, Arthur and Hannah had to end their tour, having seen only about a quarter of the house. Arthur knows it well, and was delighted to have come back to show the magnificent work of its architect Robert Adam to Hannah. But Syon House certainly has more rooms to see and more fascinating history to tell.

The Long Gallery posed Robert Adam another problem. At 136 feet long and only 14 feet wide, it was very much the typical gallery of Elizabethan and Jacobean times. For the house which forms the shell of the present building was begun in 1547 by the Duke of Somerset, Protector of the Realm on the accession of the young King Edward VI. Somerset did not have long to enjoy his new possession: his enemies had him charged with felony and executed five years later. The entire history of the house is interlinked with events of national importance, often connected with deaths and imprisonments. Syon had originally been a monastery with a charter signed in 1415. Soon after, it moved from Twickenham to a site in the present Syon Park – in fact to the exact spot where in 54 BC Caesar's forces had crossed the Thames and defeated the British leader Cassivellaunus. Here the monastery prospered, until the reign of Henry VIII when the monks and nuns were charged with pretty well every known sin, and the monastery was dissolved in 1539. One of the priests chose not to acknowledge the king's supremacy over the Church, and was hung, drawn and quartered for his stand; the Roman Catholic Church has since beatified him as a martyr.

Henry VIII's fifth wife, Catherine Howard, was confined at Syon for about three months before she was beheaded in 1542. And when Henry himself died five years later, his coffin lay at Syon for a night on its journey from Westminster to Windsor. A grotesque prophecy was then fulfilled. Back in 1535 a Franciscan friar, preaching before the king, had announced 'that God's judgements were ready to fall upon his head . . . and that the dogs would lick his blood as they had done Ahab's'. During its night at Syon the coffin burst open and dogs were found in the morning licking up some remains which had fallen to the floor. This was seen as divine judgement upon the King for desecrating the monastery.

The nuns at least returned to Syon for a short time but the order now lives at Syon Abbey in Devon, after over two centuries of sanctuary in Portugal. In 1594 Queen Elizabeth gave Syon to Henry Percy, 9th Earl of Northumberland, after he had donated large sums to fit out ships of war at the time of the Armada. He had an eventful life subsequently, and having helped James I to the throne found himself framed, tried by the Court of the Star Chamber, sentenced to a fine of £30,000 (which he did not have), and imprisoned for life. His crime? A distant kinsman, a conspirator in the Gunpowder Plot, happened to be dining at Syon on 4 November 1605 when a messenger called him to London. This kinsman duly went off with the messenger, who happened to be called Guy Fawkes – and the next day the plot was discovered. Northumberland was released as an act of clemency on the king's fifty-fifth birthday. From then until the death of the 11th Earl brought about the extinction of the earldom, the earls of Northumberland owned Syon. It then passed by marriage to the 6th Duke of Somerset, a descendant of the man who built it. But when the 7th Duke inherited, he gave it to his daughter and son-in-law, Sir Hugh Smithson. The earldom of Northumberland was revived for him and he later advanced to a dukedom. From him the present line of dukes is directly descended and it was thanks to him also that Robert Adam came to Syon and substantially rebuilt its interior.

Which brings us back to the old Long Gallery. Adam's solution to the problem of how to give it an illusion of width was to construct no fewer than sixty-two pilasters in groups along its length. He then designed cross lines diagonally down the ceiling, which tend to expand its apparent width. By clever groupings of the pilasters along the wall facing the window, he created a number of points of interest – for Adam, as previously noted, intended this room for the ladies to withdraw to, and described the gallery as 'finished in a style to afford variety and amusement'. It is certainly intricately decorated. All the pilasters were painted by Michelangelo Pergolesi, and below the cornice are landscapes by Francesco Zuccarelli, a founder member of the Royal Academy, along with a number of medallions containing portraits including the Emperor Charlemagne and his descendants the earls and dukes of Northumberland.

The Print Room, however, forms part of a programme of alterations commissioned by the 3rd Duke after he succeeded in 1817. The north range of Syon had remained virtually untouched by Robert Adam, despite the years he spent bringing about his grand plan for the house, and this side was not altered until the nineteenth century. The Print Room ceiling dates from 1864, when the 3rd Duke's brother Algernon, by then the 4th Duke, commissioned Monteroli to execute it.

In the West Corridor is an oak stake, a remnant of the palisade erected by the ancient Britons in the hope of stopping Julius Caesar crossing the Thames; as we have seen, that hope was a vain one. Nearby in the well of the staircase is a Sèvres vase which was presented in 1825 to the 3rd Duke by the French King Charles X, after the duke had attended his coronation as Great Britain's Ambassador Extraordinary. The same duke built the Great Conservatory in the grounds, which are a magnificent feature of Syon, and which date from the mid-fifteenth century, when nuns of the Bridgettine Order laid out 30 acres of orchards and gardens. The grounds are a spectacular and important part of Syon, which should not be missed.

But for all this it was the handiwork of Robert Adam that Arthur brought Hannah to see and which is without doubt the major feature of Syon. Adam's architecture, his designs for every aspect of his rooms, his variety of tone within a consistency of style – these were among the most fascinating features and greatest delights for both visitors.

Left *The chest of drawers by Robert Adam, made for Syon House in Chippendale's workshops. Again, this delightful piece is inlaid with several of Adam's favourite motifs*

WILTON HOUSE

Wilton House, near Salisbury in Wiltshire, is a house Arthur Negus knows and loves well. Nor was this the first visit for Arthur's guest, David Howard, expert in porcelain and heraldry. For him the profusion of heraldic devices throughout the house and contents are a source of fascination and delight.

After a preliminary tour of the whole house, Arthur and David returned to the six State Rooms which are open to the public and for which Wilton is probably best known. Two of the six stand out in particular: the Single Cube Room, so named because its dimensions are equal, 30 feet by 30 feet by 30 feet; and the adjoining Double Cube Room, which has the same height and width but is twice the length. It was to these rooms that Arthur and David gave particular attention, beginning with the smaller room.

The first feature that took Arthur's eye in the Single Cube Room, originally known as the 'withdrawing-room', was the fire-place, carved out of solid marble. It incorporates many of the motifs that appear elsewhere in the decoration of the room, in particular egg-and-tongue moulding, a lion motif (the lion is, as David Howard noted, one of the 'supporters' of the Herbert arms), lover's knots and simulated drapery. Various types of classical pediment appear above the many doors and Arthur noticed a drawing by Inigo Jones that was probably done for one of the doors in this room.

It is generally thought that Inigo Jones designed both this and the Double Cube Room shortly after a fire which devastated Wilton House in 1647. But this notion is not unchallenged, and the story of the early days of Wilton House is fascinating enough to warrant telling. Buildings have stood on the site since the eighth century, when King Egbert established a priory. Then, around 871, Wilton became an abbey as King Alfred granted land and manors to the Church. Although it later flourished as one of the three chief abbeys in the country, by 1500 it had 'dwindled

Right *The south and east façades of Wilton House. The south front is particularly magnificent, and was used as a model for other great Anglo-Palladian mansions*

48

Left *The Single Cube Room, with its magnificent ceiling by Giuseppe Cesari. The marble fire-place echoes decorative motifs which recur throughout the house; its similarity in shape to the double doors, with their broken pediments, is immediately clear*

Above right *The double-sided desk by William Vile – solid, ornate and superb. The top is in quarters, each of which opens out to create an area twice the size. It is photographed here not in the Single Cube Room, but in the Private Library*

Right *A close-up of the William Vile desk, which reveals just how cleverly the line of fluting conceals the keyhole to one of the secret drawers. The lion's mask monopodium on the right is an impressive piece of carving*

down to a house of moderate dimensions'. In 1544 it was somewhat derelict when King Henry VIII made a present of it to William Herbert, a wild and extravagant character who was to become 1st Earl of Pembroke, and about whom we shall hear more. He consulted his friend, the court artist Hans Holbein, and asked him to design Wilton anew, but the only elements that survive today are the centre of the east front, and a building known as the 'Holbein porch', which has since been banished to the gardens.

If Holbein's Tudor house suited the 1st Earl, it clearly did not satisfy the 4th Earl, Philip. Around 1633 he commissioned a man called Isaac de Caux to make alterations and add an immense formal garden. This he began to do, probably advised by Inigo Jones, who was then working for Charles I at Greenwich. De Caux completed at least the south front, including the State Rooms, but didn't get much further. Philip meanwhile was nimbly changing sides in the Civil War, and succeeded by so doing in preserving his estates. He may have wondered why he bothered, for in 1647 came the fire which destroyed most of the house and its contents. Inigo Jones was immediately brought in to rebuild it, even more sumptuously than before, but he was old, and his assistant and nephew John Webb went on to complete the work. The work of de Caux and then Jones includes a south front that is so magnificent that it became the model for several great Anglo-Palladian mansions, and a set of State Rooms that are among the finest of their kind in England. And all this was created in the difficult political climate of civil war and the triumph of Puritanism – which apparently never quite reached Wilton!

But how much of what remains is by de Caux and how much by Jones? As we have seen, Arthur pointed out Jones's drawing for a door in the Single Cube Room, but the central space of the ceiling boasts a fine painting of *Daedalus and Icarus* by Giuseppe Cesari, who died in 1640, before the fire at Wilton. The existence of the painting indicates that some of de Caux's rooms survived the fire at least partially, and that Inigo Jones was not faced with a complete reconstruction.

If the structure of the Single Cube Room is of uncertain ancestry, then its furniture definitely is not – and two pieces here proved to be of particular interest to Arthur. The first, one of Arthur's favourite pieces in the house, is sometimes kept out of public view in the library but on this visit graced a corner of the Single Cube Room. It is a double-sided desk by William Vile. As Arthur noted, Vile died in 1767, so he was a contemporary of England's most famous furniture-maker, Thomas Chippendale. When David Howard asked how the two compared, Arthur's answer was that many sources rate Vile as Chippendale's equal, and that he does too. Vile was in fact highly regarded in his own day, working for a considerable time as cabinet-maker to King George III. Certainly this desk is solid and magnificent, and Arthur's admiration for it was clear. Vile loved to carve deep and impressive supports on his furniture, often with cherub heads or, as here, lion masks. The top of the desk is in quarters, each of which opens out to create an area double the size. Originally it would have boasted a leather surface with gilt tooling round the edges. Just below the top is a line of decorative vertical fluting, with carved flower-heads and two concealed keyholes for secret drawers. The skill of the concealment and the inventiveness of the idea are both remarkable. When Arthur removed one of the drawers, it looked as if it had not been used for about 100 years. He sums the desk up as 'a most important piece of English furniture'.

Right in the centre of the Single Cube Room stands the other piece of furniture that Arthur especially liked – a magnificent Regency table. It is solid and ornate, with carved dolphins forming the base which is the most intricate element, and extravagant gold leaf on the carvings. The octagonal table-top itself is relatively plain, probably made from oak grown on the Wilton estate. It has an ebony band inlaid with brass shaped in leaves and flower-heads around the edge; otherwise it is undecorated. All the rest of the furniture in the room, including the settees and chairs, is from the Regency period.

Photographs of the Herbert family are often displayed on the big table, but on this occasion there was a pair of English silver candlesticks and porcelain from the Vienna service, more of which is permanently on view in the Great Ante-Room. The candlesticks are by John Schofield, and carry the London date letter for 1796, while the detachable nozzles bear that for the year 1797. Date marks are like car registrations – the letter changes part-way through the year. So, as Arthur explained, if the candlesticks were made in March 1796 and the nozzles in June of

the same year they would carry different date letters in their hallmarks. The candlesticks carry the Herbert crest and a coronet. The porcelain, made a decade later, bears the same crest and coronet within the ribbon of the Order of the Garter, which had been awarded to the 11th Earl of Pembroke. As David remarked, it is curious that the Viennese should have been able to make a porcelain service for an English family at that time – for 1807, the year of manufacture, saw Europe in the grip of the Napoleonic Wars. (Only two years earlier Napoleon had defeated the combined Russian and Austrian armies at Austerlitz.) But the service was duly completed and it contains several unusual pieces. The 'monteith', for instance, is a large oval two-handled bowl with the top rim cut in the shape of a parapet. It was invented late in the seventeenth century and was filled with ice so that wineglasses could rest in it and be cooled. But why call it a monteith? It was so named after the contemporary Scottish Earl of Monteith, who used to wear a cape that was designed with sections cut out of the bottom hem.

The Herbert arms, which appear on the candlesticks and Vienna service, can also be seen in the decoration of the Single Cube Room, as in many rooms here. Arthur noticed that there are even small cast-brass armorials on the walls, which on close examination turn out to be

Left *Various pieces from the Vienna service. The monteith in the foreground would have been filled with ice so that wineglasses could be rested in it to cool, supported by the parapet-shaped rim*

Right *The spectacular Double Cube Room, looking towards the vast painting by Van Dyck of the 4th Earl of Pembroke with his wife and children. The coved plaster portion of the ceiling visible here was painted in about 1635 by Edward Pierce; the red velvet settees are the work of William Kent*

Left *One of William Kent's tables in the Double Cube Room. This one boasts a marble top and a deep frieze featuring a mask head and scrolls, and dates from about 1740*

Right *One of the garniture of vases by Samson, dating from 1895. The crescent, symbol of the second son of an earl, can clearly be seen between the three lions; but so can the coronet above it, which signifies that the holder of the coronet is an earl*

bell-pushes for summoning a servant – a very cunning piece of design. The arms themselves show three lions on a half-blue, half-red background. David explained that the 1st Earl was a military man, and lions are an appropriate martial emblem; he spent time in France as well as England, which may account for the blue background as well as the red.

He was by all accounts an extraordinary personality. As a soldier, described in one source as a 'mad fighting young fellow', he won favour with King Henry VIII for his courage and wit. 'Black Will' (as he became known) was formidable but deeply loved at least by his dog, which gazes adoringly at his master in a portrait at Wilton. Will was also politically astute enough to hold high offices under Henry, Edward VI (of whom he was guardian), Mary and Elizabeth. His motto, painted around the Single Cube Room among others, confirms this skill in statesmanship: *Ung Je Serviray*. It may well be that it was to reassure Henry VIII of his allegiance that he chose a motto that means 'I Will Serve But One' – referring to his king. That is David Howard's opinion, but the late 16th Earl considered that the 'one' referred to God. Perhaps Black

Will deliberately chose to be ambiguous. High on the wall above the fire-place is a fine six-quartered shield that also testifies to the 1st Earl's foresight – or his extreme good luck. For the shield depicts various aspects of the Herbert lineage, and features in particular the Parr family. Black Will married Anne Parr, sister to the Catherine who later married and survived King Henry. As David pointed out, that had the useful effect of making the earl brother-in-law to his monarch.

The Herbert family still owns Wilton, sixteen generations later, and some of the other earls have also been unusually astute. In the late seventeenth century, for instance, Thomas, the 8th Earl, smuggled an enormous cask labelled 'Canary wine' into the country from France. When it reached Wilton out stepped two of the King of France's most skilled weavers! It was under their tuition that the world-famous manufacture of Wilton carpets, which still flourishes today, was founded.

Returning to the sixteenth century, the earl had a rather more conventional notion of patronage. Thanks to the Renaissance and to Henry VIII's enlightenment on the subject, the court had become the major patron of all the

for the philosopher's stone. Tradition has it that shortly after the 2nd Earl died Shakespeare came here to give the first performance of either *Twelfth Night* or *As You Like It* (tradition seems unsure which one). Certainly the first folio edition of his plays, published in 1623, was dedicated to 'the most noble and incomparable pair of brethren', the 3rd and 4th earls. Thanks to all this Wilton has been described as 'the most important house in the art history of England'.

Through this tradition of patronage, noble families also supported major artists and craftsmen. As a result, some houses gained exceptional items of furniture (the William Vile desk is one example) or, more frequently, paintings. Henry VIII had employed Hans Holbein as court painter. At Wilton, the 'incomparable' 4th Earl, Philip, commissioned Sir Anthony Van Dyck to paint a series of great family portraits to adorn the main room of the grand new house he was having designed. This room, despite the fire, eventually turned into the Double Cube Room. It has been described as 'probably the most beautiful room in any house in this country'; Charles II called it 'the best proportioned room' he knew. Arthur and David's reactions upon entering the room were also ones of admiration, not simply for the scale and for the portraits, but also for the way the Double Cube echoes the decorative motifs seen in the Single Cube Room, from flowers and lover's knots to the profusion of 'HPM' monograms that are found almost everywhere around the house. The 4th Earl was granted the earldom of Montgomery, so from his time onwards the family has been the Herberts of Pembroke and Montgomery: hence the initials HPM.

The first of the nine Van Dyck portraits that Arthur and David stopped to look at dominates the west wall, and is no less than 17 feet wide. Remembering who commissioned the artist it is perhaps no surprise that it depicts Philip, 4th Earl, with his second wife and children (three children who had died are shown as angels in the top left-hand corner). Also in the picture is a vast shield which intrigued David Howard – it tells a fascinating history of the family in the various heraldic motifs and quarterings.

In a room of this magnificence, it takes some particularly fine furniture to stand comparison. Arthur and David looked first at a 17-foot-long Regency settee, which sits below the great family group painting, and runs its full length. In scale and extravagance of decoration it is well

arts, in England as elsewhere in Europe. Art was secular and fashionable. Noblemen went to Henry's (and later Elizabeth's) court and saw the way the arts were encouraged and patronised; they then returned to their country houses, and did likewise. The 2nd Earl had a head start by marrying Mary Sidney, sister to Sir Philip Sidney, and Wilton House soon became renowned for its patronage of the stage and literature. According to John Aubrey it was 'like a college, there were so many learned and ingeniose persons'. Philip Sidney wrote his *Arcadia* there, and scenes from it are depicted in a set of pictures below the dado rail which runs at chair-back level round the Single Cube Room. Edmund Spenser, Philip Massinger, Ben Jonson and Samuel Daniel were frequent visitors, as apparently were chemists, horse-breeders, entomologists, and searchers

Right *The Upper Cloisters, designed by the notorious James Wyatt around the turn of the nineteenth century. In the foreground stands one of the footman's chairs whose central oval contains the crest of the Buller family; it dates from 1780-90*

Left *The Colonnade Room, divided by its row of Ionic columns. Andien de Clermont's bizarrely decorated ceiling forms a strange contrast with the sumptuous and solid-looking wall decoration*

garniture of vases, a set David Howard knows well. At first sight it appears to be Chinese *famille verte*, from the early eighteenth century. But, in fact, it was made in Paris in 1895 by one M. Samson – the clues are in the coat of arms painted on all the pieces. Between the three lions is a crescent – the symbol of a second son. But above this the earl's coronet is painted, so the arms show Lord Pembroke to be both earl and younger brother of an earl at the same time. Clearly, when Sidney Herbert succeeded his brother George in 1895, he assumed the earl's coronet, but forgot to remove the junior emblem of the crescent. More curious still is the *jardinière* from this set, as David recounted. It was never ordered by the Pembrokes. In fact, the late Lady Pembroke spotted it in Paris before the last war, and bought it. It appears that the mischievous Samson made up a number of orders for the English nobility, and when he saw a design he particularly liked, he ran off a few more to sell privately elsewhere!

Though Arthur and David looked at various other items from around the house, the Single and Double Cube Rooms were the only two rooms they had time to see in any detail. Arthur's final exhortation was that the visitor should come and see how much more the house has to offer, and at Wilton that is no small amount.

There are four other State Rooms to see, each of which houses a number of fine paintings. The two smaller ones, the Corner Room and the Little Ante-Room, are veritable picture galleries. And there is some fine furniture. The Corner Room houses chairs designed by Robert Adam, which were made in the Chippendale workshops, as well as two eighteenth-century French commodes. The Little Ante-Room features settees and chairs by Chippendale and Kent. Another State Room, the Colonnade Room, has some Kent furniture, two superb writing-tables from around 1700 by Boulle and another from the same period by Jensen. This room is quite remarkable; it takes its name from the row of four Ionic columns that divides it, an appealing and unusual feature. Equally unusual, but thought by some to be not at all appealing, is the ceiling, which was painted nearly a century after the room was finished, between 1735 and 1739. Above solidly grand wall decoration in the style of the two cube rooms, Andien de Clermont painted a light and exotic design, featuring tropical birds and monkeys, that creates a bizarre and incongruous effect.

suited to this vast room; it is also upholstered in the patterned red of the rug. There are mirrors and footstools made by Thomas Chippendale, which are as immaculate today as they were when they were made in 1760, and there are no fewer than six settees in red velvet by William Kent, dating from about 1740. Arthur was particularly taken with the typically ornate decoration they display, with mask heads, fish scales, even a pair of mermaids forming a gilded frieze between the legs. The solidity and extravagance of these Kent designs seem to fit perfectly into a room of this character. Clearly, the Herberts thought so too, for there are also four exquisitely carved tables designed by Kent, painted in white and gold, with marble tops. Arthur spent some time looking at these, and noted the typical deep frieze and inverted 'S'-shaped legs.

Armorial porcelain is displayed on the tables. On this occasion there were a number of pieces from the 'Samson'

Right *The Palladian bridge, with the south façade of the house in the background. It was designed in 1737 by the 9th Earl of Pembroke, who was an architect of some note, and his assistant Roger Morris*

These State Rooms are connected by the Gothic Upper Cloisters, added when the 11th Earl commissioned James Wyatt in 1801 to alter Wilton in order to make it warmer and more convenient. Before the cloisters were built, you had to pass through every room to traverse the house as there were no corridors. Wyatt made several major alterations. He pulled down the previous north and west fronts to make way for his new arrangement, which greets the visitor today. He banished the fine Holbein porch to the garden, added an entrance porch which has since been demolished, and swept away the west rooms to make way for a library – the ceiling of which fell down in the 1930s.

In fact collapsing ceilings were one of the trademarks of the extraordinary Wyatt, whose career was colourful in the extreme. In the late eighteenth century he supplanted Robert Adam as the most fashionable architect of the day.

He took over 200 commissions and travelled over 4,000 miles a year on business. He worked in many styles, from Adamesque, to Roman, to neoclassical (we shall see some of his work in this style at Goodwood House) – but his favourite was Gothic, as at Wilton. Highly talented though he was, people loved to hate him. His remodelling of the House of Lords, for instance, was described as 'beastly bad taste' and was even likened to 'a gentlemen's lavatory'.

But the real anger Wyatt aroused was reserved for his working methods. He took on huge amounts of work but was too disorganised to cope with it. He dashed round the country to see his clients, was never punctual, mostly infuriated them, and later in life became known for eating and drinking heavily when he did eventually arrive and for falling asleep at table or at meetings. His work at Wilton

cloisters. The Upper Cloisters contain paintings, furniture, porcelain and other items, two of which Arthur and David Howard stopped to look at. Arthur's eye was caught by a 'footman's' chair with an oval back containing nine smaller ovals, dating from 1780-90. The crest in the central oval was identified by David as that of the Buller family, who were prominent in Devon and Cornwall at the time. As Arthur explained, one of these chairs would be placed outside all the principal rooms in the house, for the footman to sit upon, ready to attend to his master. David noticed one of the pairs of Chinese jars that adorn the cloisters. They are excellent – decorated in blue and white, and displaying a favourite motif of the Chinese, the phoenix. Although previously thought to have been made in the eighteenth century, David identified them as from the Chinese 'transitional' period, which would date them to around 1635. Thus they could have been bought new, to go with the contemporary rebuilding of the State Rooms.

Two final rooms are worth mentioning before leaving Wilton: the Little and Large Smoking Rooms. They form part of the Inigo Jones and John Webb house and have retained much of their splendour. Apart from paintings they also have some fine furniture: the Little Smoking Room houses a rare set of walnut pieces with floral marquetry comprising mirror, table and pair of stands dating from around 1670. The larger room boasts some bookcases, and one of Arthur's favourite pieces at Wilton: an exceptional bureau cabinet made for the house in about 1750 by Thomas Chippendale. It features an exquisitely carved violin in the door decoration: a worthy piece to conclude with.

So, as Arthur said, there is much to see at Wilton House. Of greatest interest are the six State Rooms, among which the magnificent Double Cube Room is pre-eminent. But the house's history, represented in its unbroken line of family succession, and reflected in its architectural travails and triumphs, fine furniture and collection of art-historical treasures, is absorbing and enlightening throughout. And it would be as wrong to omit here as it would be for the visitor to omit to see the vast garden to the south with its lawns, cedars, delightful Palladian bridge and crowning view of the south and east façades of the house. Looking at it, it is easy to see why Wilton House became the model for so many other great mansions.

was certainly not his most auspicious. Apart from the library, all the woodwork in the new cloisters was found to be infected with dry rot; the chimneys caught fire the first time they were used and the new roof leaked and had to be entirely rebuilt. Lord Pembroke's rage at Wyatt still burns across the centuries, in explosive correspondence. Wyatt died in 1813 in a coach accident, apparently driving at great speed from one client to another. By now he was in penury, not through lack of commissions nor extravagance, but because he was too disorganised (or generous-spirited) to claim his fees. At his death he was owed more than £20,000, including £1,000, apparently, by Wilton House. That's in the order of £2 million in today's terms, with Wilton owing a cool £100,000.

Having said all that, what remains of Wyatt's work at Wilton is not displeasing, in the Gothic Hall, staircase and

FIRLE PLACE

'A house overflowing with fine porcelain, particularly Sèvres, and fine furniture.' This was Arthur's opening description of Firle Place, where he came in company with David Battie, a friend and expert on ceramics from a major auction house. Firle is a Tudor house and park lying just east of Lewes in Sussex, under the steep northern slopes of the Downs. Like many houses it has undergone structural change, and now looks outwardly Georgian, although it retains its early Tudor courtyard building. Seen from the park, it is sheltered by great beech trees which beautifully complement the creamy-white stonework.

Arthur summarised the collections of pictures, porcelain and furniture at Firle Place as being characteristic of a family that has been in residence for 500 years, with each generation buying, as it went, according to the styles of the times. Apart from missals and drawings there is, however, little of the Tudor fittings and possessions left, although a 30-foot-long 'Tudor Roll' has been found. It belonged to a religious order and includes an inventory of how Firle Place was furnished at the time. There were among other things 'a drawinge table of walnutt tree, two liverye cupboards, two wanscott formes, a shovell board table and frame' and much more besides.

The Gage family, which has owned Firle for so long, hailed originally from Normandy. In 1066 a feudal lord called de Gaugi came to England with William the Conqueror, fought the good fight, and was given land near Gloucester. And there he lived, having done his bit. His descendant, Sir John Gage, moved to Sussex when he married Eleanor St Clere, whose family were large landowners in the Firle district. His grandson, also called Sir John Gage, almost certainly enlarged Firle Place in early Tudor times, probably on the site of an earlier building.

This Sir John was astute enough to be a staunch Catholic and still stay in favour with Henry VIII, who made him

Left *Sheltered by the trees: a delightful view of Firle Place*

called Lady Penelope Darcy, who had two other suitors at the same time. She told them that if they had patience she would marry each of them in turn; she must have been clairvoyante, because that's what she did. Her first husband died after a few months. She then married John, who died in 1633 after twenty-two years, upon which, after a suitable pause, she took up with suitor number three. Portraits of Lady Penelope and her three husbands hang in the Staircase Hall at Firle.

But it was in the Drawing Room upstairs that Arthur and David began looking at the treasures on display. Arthur went first to a Louis XVI commode, dating from around 1770 and mounted with fine French ormolu. They both admired its beautifully tooled ormolu flower-heads, Vitruvian or convoluted scrolls, and marquetry panels made of different coloured veneers featuring satinwood flowers, tied with ribbons. It has three shallow drawers on

Left *One of the* tricoteuses *in the Upstairs Drawing Room, with its trellis-pattern inlay. On it is the delightful Sèvres bachelor early morning tea service dating from 1761, painted in several bright colours*

one of his executors. He was clearly a good strategist, both military and political, for he was captain of the royal guard before commanding the expedition which ended in the death of James V of Scotland at Solway Moss. He also found time to be Vice-Chamberlain to the king and later, having had the nerve to disapprove of the king's divorce, became Constable of the Tower, Comptroller of the Household and Chancellor of the Duchy of Lancaster.

His son fared less fortunately, landing, as Sheriff of Sussex, the unpleasant job of superintending the burning of the Lewes martyrs; but *his* son was unluckier still. By now it was not the safest possible course to declare yourself a Catholic. John Gage did so, and was twice thrown in jail for 'obstinacy in popery'. He died in 1598, to be succeeded by his nephew, also – predictably – called John Gage.

This John Gage chose to fall in love with a young lady

Right *The Upstairs Drawing Room. Over the fire-place hangs Fra Bartolommeo's* Holy Family, *often considered his most beautiful work. All the paintings are in fact Italian, and came from Panshanger; the furniture is mostly French*
Top right *One of the two 'Panshanger Cabinets' thought to be by Thomas Chippendale, in the style of Robert Adam. The superb ormolu mounts are probably the work of Matthew Boulton*

top, and two deep ones below. This is a very fine commode and, as we shall see later, the Long Gallery has two even finer ones which are not quite what they seem.

Close to the commode is one of a pair of little French tray-like tables. Arthur stopped to admire the exquisite workmanship in a trellis-pattern inlay on both table-top and under-tier. The front edge of the tray can be lowered on hinges. As Arthur explained, it is not simply a tray, but a little work-table called a *tricoteuse*, so needlework or embroidery could have been put on it. It is one of many small, elaborate French pieces in this room which represent a move, in the mid-eighteenth century, from grand and formal reception rooms to more intimate, private apartments where the furniture was smaller and more comfortable. On the table on the day of Arthur's visit was a small bachelor early-morning tea service, meant for just one person. David Battie set the scene: 'How would you

like to have your tea served from one of these in your French château in your sumptuous four-poster bed?' For it is an exceptional set of Sèvres porcelain dated 1761, in unusual and lively colours. What's more, it features the same pattern design as the table, with which it is contemporary – proof that fashionable designs were used on whatever kind of material was suitable.

Talking of fashionable designs, there are two huge display cabinets, known as the 'Panshanger Cabinets', in the upper Drawing Room. They are glass-fronted, with elaborate marquetry and very unusual concave ends; the decoration is effected in motifs published by Thomas Hope. There are huge round medallions, with husks falling from them, and on each of the frontal doors below the glass a large urn, brimming with swags of foliage. These are some of the most ambitious pieces of work in this style: all in all, as Arthur said, marvellous. They have fine ormolu mounts with motifs including husks, rams' heads and acanthus leaves. Like the French furniture in the room, they were formerly in the collection of the Cowper family, at their Panshanger home, but when the late 6th Viscount married Imogen Grenfell in 1931 she brought her inheritance with her, including some of the finest paintings, furniture and porcelain now at Firle.

Moving across the room, Arthur and David came to an octagonal porcelain dish set on an octagonal table. The table is of considerable size, but when he looked at it Arthur noticed that the top was made of a single sheet of mahogany veneer. It must, as he remarked, have come from a huge tree. Sadly, it shows a lighter patch near one corner; Arthur diagnosed this as a loss of colour due to the table having been left by a window too long. Clearly some rain water had seeped in, and damaged the table. David asked whether a flaw like that could be removed, to be told that in the hands of a good restorer it could be brought back to its original state.

David identified the piece of porcelain on the table as a dish from the East India Company, dating from the middle of the eighteenth century. Firle Place does not only boast French porcelain, though its Sèvres collection is excellent – it also has English and Chinese pieces, among others, and this example, painted with a goose and a peony, is an attractive piece from the Orient. As if to point out how universal certain favoured patterns became, its pink border is decorated in a style that echoes the pattern we saw earlier on the work-table and tea set.

David and Arthur then came to the second work-table of the pair, to find upon it a piece of English porcelain. David described it as a first period Worcester chestnut basket, dating from 1775. It is decorated with a pretty spray of flowers, just like the design on a porcelain plaque mounted in the top of a small French table that stands next to it. This is another piece of furniture intended for a private apartment and the plaque this time is Sèvres. Arthur and David stopped to admire it before moving on.

Downstairs is another Drawing Room; it was formerly the dining room, and in the nineteenth century a music room. Like most of the rooms in the house, it was rebuilt in Georgian times. The work was commenced by Sir William Gage, perhaps shortly after he came of age in 1716. He, like Arthur Negus, was fond of cricket, and was one of its earliest devotees among the Sussex gentry. In

Right *The Long Gallery at Firle Place: it is unusual to find such a room introduced into a house as late as the mid-eighteenth century, as this was. None the less it is a very fine room, housing some excellent paintings and objects*

Far right *Against the wall, though not in the Long Gallery where Arthur and David saw it, is the delightful and intricate George II kneehole desk – not English or Dutch, but from Goa*

1735 he captained a Gentlemen of Sussex eleven against the Gentlemen of Kent, led by the Earl of Middlesex, in a match at Sevenoaks.

The downstairs Drawing Room of Thomas, 1st Viscount Gage is unusual, with three compartments, divided by balancing screens with Ionic columns. It contains, apart from some gilt side-tables, a set of chairs particularly admired by Arthur and attributed to Thomas Chippendale in about 1765. He showed David one of the armchairs. It is in the style called Chinese Chippendale, with an open lattice back. At the top of the chair-back is a carved thistle, indicating that the set of eight was probably originally made for a Scotsman. Unusually, this chair does not have pierced fretwork under the arms, although the supports to the arms themselves are pierced – this also is rare.

On the walls are six full-length portraits, including one by Gainsborough of the 2nd Viscount, William Hall Gage, who was born in 1718. He was, apparently, a genial but absent-minded man, who loved Firle passionately and was afraid his successors might some day desert it for Highmeadow, his mother's home in Gloucestershire.

According to a letter probably written by the 3rd Viscount he 'systematically destroyed the Grounds, Gardens and Premises' at Highmeadow 'with a view to prevent his successors from ever living there', quite an act of vandalism, whatever the motive. Another portrait depicts General Thomas Gage, who was Commander-in-Chief in North America, and at the outbreak of the War of Independence was Governor of Massachusetts. He it was who, in 1775, directed the Battle of Bunker Hill and became the object of bitter reproach. Modern American authorities now disagree with this judgement of him, for the British government sent only 6,000 reinforcements instead of the 32,000 requested by the general to combat the 15,000 besiegers of Boston.

His extraordinary uncle was Joseph Gage, Count of Spain and a general in the Spanish army. He had a fantastic career. First he made a fortune in Paris by investing in Mississippi stock, spent much time at the French court, and became an intimate friend of Louis XV. He then offered the kings of Poland and Sardinia in turn a cool £3 million for their crowns. Having failed to buy either,

he lost all his money when the South Sea Bubble burst, so he went to Madrid, was granted a silver mine, was made a grandee and given command of the Spanish army in Italy. From 1743 to 1746 he fought the Austrians there, and was awarded a pension of 4,000 ducats as a gesture of appreciation by the king of Naples. There is no painting of him in the Lower Drawing Room, but the frivolous among us may wonder how history might have been rewritten, had we had Joseph at Bunker Hill instead of his nephew!

Back upstairs in the Long Gallery, the first thing David and Arthur stopped to look at was another portrait – by Allan Ramsay, of George III, painted some fifteen years after he came to the throne, showing him dressed in magnificent robes and ermine. This is also, as Arthur noted, a Georgian room, but unusual in that, although long galleries are common features in Elizabethan and Jacobean houses, it is rare to find one introduced in the middle of the eighteenth century. It extends the full length of the first floor of the entrance front, and seems to have been built, despite its old-fashioned form, to house the 1st

Viscount's collection of paintings. The work for the Georgian phase was started by Sir William Gage between 1713 and 1744, and completed by Thomas, 1st Viscount, between 1744 and 1754. He probably used a local family of masons, Arthur and John Morris, who also worked on other country houses such as Stanmer and Compton Place, Eastbourne.

Looking round, it was clear to Arthur and David why such a major room was needed to house all the collection. Even so, Arthur's eye was drawn first to an object that does not always live in the gallery – a delightful small George II knee-hole desk. It has highly coloured seventeenth-century marquetry panels depicting birds and flowers; but it is not English. Nor despite appearances is it Dutch. A quick way Arthur used to discover this was to look at a drawer – the drawer sides were not nailed, so it was not Dutch. The drawers are lined with padouk, a well-marked type of rosewood from the Burmese area, for the desk is in fact Indo-Portuguese, from Goa. Opening the top drawer Arthur discovered small, ornate drawers fitted with compartments for razors, powders and suchlike for, although it looks like a simple writing-desk, it is in fact a knee-hole writing/dressing-table.

On the wall above it Arthur pointed out one of the oval Chippendale mirrors, in carved wood and gold leaf, decorated with flower-heads trailing in and out along the border. It is made more attractive by having an outer mirror border and is, as Arthur mentioned, the more valuable by being oval in shape; such mirrors are more highly regarded than rectangular ones.

From the fine porcelain collection in the room, David Battie had picked out some of his favourites. He grouped together, for Arthur to look at, a few examples of colour-ground Sèvres, collected around the turn of the century, when this kind of porcelain was very popular. From the pieces in pinks, greens and blues David particularly liked an inkstand with the porcelain figure of a lady, entwined in ormolu, as its centre. It dates from the late eighteenth century. The delightful blue ink-wells are in fact Sèvres egg-cups.

Beautiful as these pieces are, they show also that tastes change. At the turn of the century, when these items were purchased, they were at the height of their popularity and reflect the collecting taste of that time.

David observed that more fine old French porcelain has survived in England than in France. The same can be said about French furniture, the bulk of which appeared in England after the French Revolution. After the Revolution the *émigré* French nobility found they needed cash in hand, not objects and furniture. So they came to London and sold off their goods, probably quite cheaply. Those who did not flee risked the same fate as royalty in having their possessions seized. Such furniture was auctioned off in a series of sales from 1793 onwards. During the Peace of Amiens a number of Englishmen came to Paris to find much of this furniture still for sale, and more furniture continued to trickle over to England even during the Napoleonic Wars. After Waterloo, the movement of French furniture to England picked up once more, first from the again impoverished aristocracy, and then from

other suddenly destitute echelons of society. The London auction rooms profited from a long and valuable stream of fine goods coming across the Channel.

A pair of items that might have made such a journey caught Arthur's eye next – a rare pair of Régence commodes, dating from around 1725-30, described as possibly the finest pieces of furniture in the house. Arthur did not make this claim for them, although they are undoubtedly excellent. Each has a double serpentine front which, as Arthur pointed out, forms the shape of an archer's bow. They are veneered in kingwood and amaranth, with the trellis pattern we saw on the work-tables, and feature very fine ormolu, which particularly appealed to David. The form is known as *commode en tombeau*. There is one deep drawer at the bottom, and two above, but when you open the top you realise that these two are in fact simulated, and that the upper part functions as a rug chest. The interior is solid walnut, which is unusual as most such commodes are veneered on oak.

On the second commode David found a pair of Sèvres

Left *Two of the 'Firle Vases', made in 1763 by Charles Nicholas Dodin. Some of the panels feature chinoiserie subjects, which is unusual and may indicate that the vases were a royal commission*

Right *Part of the excellent Sèvres 'Melbourne Service', made in 1771 for the 1st Lord Melbourne. It was extremely expensive when made, but is considered one of the finest examples of Sèvres in this country*

Above *A Chinese Ch'ien Lung hawk in biscuit porcelain. The painstakingly painted feathers were brushed directly onto the porcelain, which is unglazed*
Left *The pair of Japanese Imari porcelain hounds which particularly appealed to Arthur*

Right *A painting of Firle Place, dating from 1827, depicting an occasion when the traditional sport of tilting at a quintain was revived. Contemporary newspaper accounts recorded the event: three quintains (movable targets) were hung from poles, and one contestant is seen charging to tilt while another rides off in the opposite direction. A 'cold collation of upwards of 300 dishes' was served afterwards*

vases, two of the very finest pieces in the collection and known as the 'Firle Vases'. As Arthur remarked, in this house everything seems to come in pairs. While it isn't unusual for such items to be made this way, it is quite rare for both parts to survive and stay together. Looking at the base of one vase, David found enough marks to give him quite a lot of information. There is the 'K' mark dating it to 1763, and a smaller 'k' below which attributes it to a particular maker – Charles Nicholas Dodin. There is also the genuine mark of Sèvres, which is quite uncommon as fakes of this date abound; it displays the royal monogram of two interlaced 'L's, granted by Louis XV in 1753. Louis had for some time been fond of porcelain, and he was patron of a company formed between 1738 and 1745 to produce soft-paste porcelain which was made from ground glass and white clay rather than the china clay and china rock used for hard-paste porcelain. About thirty years earlier, no one in the west had succeeded in making hard-paste porcelain at all, although the secret had long been discovered by the Chinese and Japanese, who exported porcelain as early as the Middle Ages. Hence Louis's interest. The company was at first installed in the royal castle at Vincennes, and in 1753 given the title of Manufacture Royale de Porcelaines de France. Three years later the factory moved to larger premises at Sèvres, just outside Paris, and the king became the sole shareholder.

Sèvres is generally reckoned to be the finest and most elegant of eighteenth-century European porcelains, appreciated in particular for the softness of its white glaze, and the brilliance of the many colours used. Also admired is the quality of the painting – the Dodin pair have finely pencilled oriental-style paintings on the panels. David thought that this might indicate that the vases were a royal commission; certainly chinoiserie subjects are very unusual. They may well have been closely copied from paintings on the Chinese 'eggshell' porcelain plates that were decorated for the European market at Canton a few years earlier.

David also picked out from the cabinets a set of plates from the 'Melbourne Service', made at Sèvres for the 1st Lord Melbourne in 1771. A bill surviving in the archive shows that the whole lot – forty-eight plates, wine coolers, tureens, and many other pieces – cost £5,500 at the time. He liked most of all the *bleu céleste* colour of the ground, which has pheasant's-eye decoration on it. Each piece was also finely painted with trophies of the arts, music and love. The set is one of the finest examples of Sèvres in England – but perhaps it ought to be, at that price!

The Long Gallery boasts more than Sèvres porcelain. On the wall David pointed to a Chinese Ch'ien Lung hawk, in pink and brown biscuit porcelain; the meticulously painted feathers were all painted directly onto the porcelain without it being glazed. Arthur especially liked the pierced rock-like base the bird stood on. But he liked even better a pair of 15-inch-high porcelain hounds standing by the fireside and looking very alert indeed. They are Japanese from the eighteenth century, with white, red, black and gilded patches – a combination known as Imari from its town of export. They are quite striking, and great favourites of Arthur's. Not many such pieces were ever made so they are indeed rarities.

Arthur and David had no time to investigate Firle further, though their visit thus far had been fairly representative of the many aspects Firle has to offer. There are other fine rooms, and more furniture, porcelain and paintings. As Arthur said, they only scratched the surface. But the English and French furniture, along with the Chinese porcelain hawks and the Japanese hounds, stuck in his memory as his best-loved pieces here, just as the outstanding Sèvres collection made the visit a delight for David Battie.

GOODWOOD HOUSE

'Glorious Goodwood' is perhaps known to many for its famous races rather than for the house itself. It was appropriate, therefore, that Arthur and his long-time colleague and guest on this occasion, Bernard Price, should begin their visit by looking at a painting of Goodwood races in 1886. As Bernard pointed out, it is very much a recognisable scene, with the grandstand and the famous hill at the back, occupied by a number of people hoping to get a free look at what was going on. The foreground also shows much of interest; Arthur, while claiming not to be a musician himself, admitted to a liking for Gilbert and Sullivan operas – and spotted in the picture both Sir Arthur Sullivan and W. S. Gilbert enjoying the day out. That year *The Mikado* was being performed in London and its composers were already celebrated people. Bernard picked out the Prince of Wales, later Edward VII, who was a frequent guest at Goodwood, and also the 6th Duke of Richmond, whose estates these were. The picture portrays a famous American as well – Henry Morton Stanley, the explorer who 'discovered' Dr Livingstone.

By this time Goodwood races had become an important event in the social calendar. They had begun in 1801 as a private event, with no hint of the glory to come. The 3rd Duke of Richmond, as Colonel of the Sussex Militia, used to organise race meetings with his officers riding against each other in Petworth Park, not far away. For some reason they were forbidden, so the duke organised a meeting on the Downs of Goodwood. The following year, 1802, the meeting was opened to the public, and throughout the nineteenth century its reputation blossomed, until it was the major event depicted here.

The picture hangs in the Long Hall, which is the core of

Left *The front portico of Goodwood House, designed by James Wyatt. The 3rd Duke of Richmond in fact commissioned him to build a huge octagon with a tower at each corner, but the cost proved so great that only three of the sides were ever completed*

the old Jacobean hunting-lodge that Goodwood once was. It was originally rebuilt in 1616–17 by the 9th Earl of Northumberland whose steward had bought it for him in 1614 while the earl was locked up in the Tower of London. The rebuilding cost £550 then and the whole house set the 1st Duke of Richmond back £4,100 when he bought it in 1697. He was the illegitimate son of Charles II and Louise de Quéroualle, and in 1675 his father gave him an impressive list of titles which had lapsed on the death of James Stuart. All at once, Charles Lennox became Duke of Richmond, Earl of March, and Baron Settrington. In the peerage of Scotland he was also created Duke of Lennox, Earl of Darnley and Baron Torbolton. He bought Goodwood to use as a hunting-lodge; and it is portrayed as such in another picture in the Long Hall.

This was painted for the 2nd Duke by John Wootton, and features in the foreground a groom standing with the horse Sheldon, which was a favourite hunter of the duke's.

Above *This painting of Goodwood races in 1886 portrays among other famous people Edward, Prince of Wales, W. S. Gilbert, Sir Arthur Sullivan and the explorer Henry Morton Stanley*
Left *A detail of the same painting, in which the 6th Duke of Richmond, owner of the estate at the time, is seen in the foreground giving a helping hand to Lady Leveson-Gower*

Right *The Long Hall at Goodwood House, created by Sir William Chambers and framed at each end by white Ionic columns. This room is the core of the original Jacobean House; Chambers preserved the front door as he found it, but now it opens into the courtyard*

In the background the old Goodwood House is visible. Bernard considered this a good horse picture executed for a man who loved to hunt and ride. The 2nd Duke acquired the mastership and hounds of the nationally famous Charlton Hunt and changed its name to the Goodwood Hunt. It survived until 1813 when the pack was wiped out by an attack of rabies. The 2nd Duke appears by all accounts to have led a fascinating life, not least in the manner of his marriage. When only eighteen he was wedded to Sarah, daughter of the Earl of Cadogan, for the most bizarre of reasons: to settle a gambling debt between the two fathers. Immediately after the ceremony he was rushed off for three years on the Grand Tour with a tutor. When he got back to England he was so uninterested in seeing his wife that he went straight to the theatre instead. There he was captivated by a lovely woman. On inquiring he was told that she was 'the reigning toast of London, the beautiful Lady March'; none other than his own wife. So he and Sarah were reunited and were married for another twenty-eight years – a fairy-tale ending to a strange true story.

Moving away from the paintings in the Long Gallery, Arthur came upon a regulator clock by John Shelton of London. Shelton was well-known through having worked as foreman to, and later taken over from, that most celebrated of clocksmiths, George Graham. This particular regulator had an interesting history: it was, as Bernard noted, brought down to Portsmouth dockyard in 1764 and used to check the famous Harrison Chronometer H4. The chronometer was tested by being sent on a voyage to the West Indies and back. It was found to have kept perfect time with this regulator (snug in Portsmouth throughout the chronometer's voyage), and this was the beginning of accurate marine time-keeping. And that, in turn, was vital if navigators were to establish their exact position at sea – which they had never been able to do before. It is a long-case regulator with a normal dial, including a subsidiary seconds dial; but standing close to it is another long-case clock whose dials are far from normal.

The 'Pendleton of London' clock, whose maker, according to Arthur, was active between 1780 and 1808, shows three dials and a crescent. There is a twenty-four-hour dial, a separate minutes dial and a separate seconds dial, but the crescent has gradations from 'D15' down to zero. This is an unusual yet very useful addition; it displays how many days there are to go before rewinding is needed. The clock itself is very grand, as Arthur pointed out; it has brass-cased weights, which is a sign of very good quality, and a little pendulum which is also cased.

Beneath the picture of the 2nd Duke's horse, Arthur

came upon a piece of furniture attributed to William Vile, one of the finest cabinet-makers of the middle of the eighteenth century (a desk by him is described in the chapter on Wilton House). This solid and grand object has a bold serpentine front. Each of the eight uprights is topped by a child's head with curly hair and chubby face, and acanthus leaves run halfway down the front. There are Vitruvian scrolls each with an extra little blossom and flower-head in the middle; all in all, as Arthur said, a lovely commode. For though there are what seem to be drawers on the front, they are, in fact, all false, and the top opens up to reveal that it is really 'one of the finest rug chests that anyone ever made'. To cap the trickery, though all the drawers are false, the lower frieze beneath them is in fact a secret drawer: nothing is what it seems. The top is, as Arthur noted, one solid piece of mahogany about 2 feet 6 inches wide, and the weight of the whole object is enormous. It has carrying handles at either end – and even they are gilt.

Bernard next came to a painting, this time of the 3rd Duke, with his wife and sister-in-law, watching the horses

Above *The 'Pendleton of London' clock, with three dials and a crescent but no conventional clock face. There is a twenty-four-hour dial, a minutes dial and a seconds dial, and the crescent indicates how many days there are to go before the clock needs to be wound again*

Above *A detail from the majestic rug chest by William Vile, showing the consummate carving of the acanthus leaves and child's head – one of Vile's favourite decorative motifs*

Right *The painting by George Stubbs of the 3rd Duke of Richmond with his wife and sister-in-law watching horses being trained on the Downs*

Right *George Stubbs's painting of a lioness snarling at the approach of a lion. Not only is this a magnificent picture, but the frame is of excellent quality too, and incorporates eight lion mask heads*

being trained on the Downs. Bernard in fact lives nearby, and was particularly impressed with the sense of topography, or map-like qualities, afforded by the painting. Looking beyond the figures, you can see the channels creeping in from the river Solent to Chichester harbour, the spire of Chichester cathedral, and in the distance you can even see as far as the Isle of Wight. Arthur very much liked the sense of movement in this painting, especially with regard to the horses. The picture by Wootton looks stiff in comparison, for this one is by no less an artist than George Stubbs, a man who, as Bernard noted, loved horses and wild animals, particularly lions.

Appropriately enough, Arthur and Bernard moved next to a Stubbs painting depicting a magnificent lioness, snarling at the approach of a somewhat mangy lion. It is signed, and dated 1771. Stubbs apparently painted at Goodwood a great deal, and perhaps got the idea for this painting from one of the 2nd Duke's more remarkable enterprises. In 1725 he created a menagerie in High Wood, the walled arboretum or tree garden behind Goodwood House. There, in underground tunnels and caverns, from which the visitors were shielded by iron bars, he kept a lion, tiger, bears, eagles and ostriches. Each day great amounts of horsemeat and other foods had to be set aside to feed them all. After dinner guests at the house would be able to walk the 300 yards to High Wood and stand on the gratings, listening to the roars of the animals. It is interesting to note that wild animals at country houses are not at all a recent innovation. The 2nd Duke must have been attached to his animals, for when the lioness died he erected a life-sized stone monument over her grave, which still stands today. Equally, the person who framed the Stubbs painting must, as Arthur noted, have been entranced by the picture. He made a carved giltwood frame, and set in it carved lion mask heads of excellent quality.

Arthur and Bernard next entered the adjacent Tapestry

Left *The Tapestry Drawing Room. This room was redesigned, probably by Wyatt, to house tapestries purchased by the 3rd Duke when he was Ambassador in Paris in 1765*

Right *One of the four magnificent Gobelins tapestries on the wall of the Tapestry Drawing Room, featuring Don Quixote and Sancho Panza. Considering their excellent detail and quality, it is not surprising that they caught the 3rd Duke of Richmond's eye*

Drawing Room, which they described as delightfully proportioned. It was the creation of the 3rd Duke of Richmond who was, among other things, Ambassador Extraordinary to the court of Louis XV at Versailles in 1765. While he was there he bought a fine collection of Sèvres porcelain, much Louis XV furniture, and a set of four Gobelins tapestries depicting the story of Don Quixote. They were made by Michael Audran and Pierre François Cozette between 1762 and 1764, after the original earlier designs of Charles Coypel, and most impressive they are, too. The room was probably reconstructed specifically to house the tapestries, and forms part of a major transformation commissioned by the 3rd Duke which turned Goodwood into the large and magnificent house it is now. To begin with, Sir William Chambers was employed in 1760 to make alterations, which included knocking the two rooms on either side of the original entrance hall into it to make one long room, which was then called the Long Hall. This hall linked the two legs of what was at the time an 'H'-shaped building. Then, towards the end of the eighteenth century, the same duke hired James Wyatt – the man whose erratic career and work are noted in the chapter on Wilton House – to carry

out a hugely ambitious plan. Wyatt was to build a massive octagon with a tower at each corner. Had the work been completed it would have created a singular and enormous house. But only three sides were ever finished, one of which was a leg of the Chambers 'H', adapted by the addition of towers. The cost was, predictably enough, astronomical, and the Duke left liabilities of some £180,000 at his death in 1806. Though criticised for some of his work elsewhere, Wyatt did however create at Goodwood a fine flint building in the neoclassical style.

The Tapestry Drawing Room was built as a drawing room alongside the Long Hall. Its magnificent ceiling, reminiscent of Robert Adam, was much admired by Bernard, who pointed out that apart from washing, it has been untouched since it was made. He was particularly amused and impressed by an odd but splendid marble fire-place by John Bacon, with male and female attendants holding furled drapery. As Bernard mentioned, Bacon was not particularly famous at the time (though he is known to have sculpted many tombs in Westminster Abbey), but he is widely admired these days. The fire-place wasn't cheap – it cost £500 then, which translates to around £30,000 today!

Arthur's eye was meanwhile taken by some of the furniture in the room, beginning with what he described as a 'very special French table', in kingwood and tulipwood. It is small and delightful, with a serpentine top inlaid with flowers. In fact, this is so fine and rare a table that a Parisian school for cabinet-makers requested photographs of it so that present-day students could learn by copying it. Arthur lifted the table in the expectation of finding a signature on the under-side – it can usually be

found on the frame – and, sure enough, there were the initials 'RVLC'. Arthur identified this as one Roger Vandercruse (alias Lacroix in France). Next to these initials were the further letters 'JME', which indicates that he was a member of the Juré de Maître Ébénistes, the governing body of the master cabinet-makers. It is rare, as Arthur noted, to find a table with such a good signature.

Close to this table stands another piece of continental furniture, for which Arthur showed some admiration, but less affection. It is an early neoclassical marquetry bureau, prolifically inlaid, and made in Germany around 1760-70, attributed to one Abraham Roentgen. As Arthur pointed out, though it isn't English it still betrays the influence of Robert Adam, particularly in its inlaid urns draped with laurel. There is a long panoramic picture in wood running the length of the bureau top, and underneath it in the centre a picture in inlay depicting the entrance hall to a mansion, and two figures standing in the foreground. All in all, it's a very elaborate piece, using walnut, satinwood, olivewood, purpleheart and applewood for the inlay, as well as ivory for the faces and hands of the figures – as Bernard interjected, a particularly continental characteristic. A fine object, but Arthur described it as a bit heavy for his own taste.

Alongside the bureau stands another table – English, this time, and also inlaid. Arthur pointed out in particular the precision of the inlay down the legs, executed in perfectly straight lines, showing great skill in the craftsmanship. It is a George III satinwood occasional table, and features an inset porcelain plaque on the top. Turning it upside-down, Bernard was able to make out on the reverse of the plaque the mark of the crossed swords – not signifying this time, as many people would immediately think, that it was a piece of Meissen, but betraying instead that it was from the English Derby factory and, according to Bernard, from around 1785-90 – about the same date as the table itself. The plaque is a picture of colourful birds, including duck and pheasant, and is a delightful piece on its own account. In fact Arthur's suspicion was that the plaque and table were not originally intended for each other at all. He reasoned that a table with such excellent inlay all down the sides and legs would be unlikely to feature on the top a porcelain plaque set in a completely plain satinwood frame. It is much more likely that the plaque was intended to be displayed on a wall, where it

Right *The George III satinwood occasional table, with a porcelain plaque inset into the top. The plain satinwood frame for the plaque can clearly be seen, in contrast to the inlaid sides and legs. The plaque is Derby, dating from around 1785-90*

Left *A small French table in kingwood and tulipwood by Roger Vandercruse. Behind it can be seen the marble fire-place by John Bacon, which features a male and a female attendant holding furled drapery*

frame the name 'L. Delanois'. He was a furniture-maker of renown, who also made furniture for Madame Du Barry, the Prince de Condé and King Stanislaus II of Poland. Because they are signed, the chairs are quite important; and in fact the loose seat-frame is signed as well as the chair-frame. Next to each signature is a number of secret marks. In the case of the chair Arthur and Bernard examined, there were four dots on the chair-frame, and also four dots on the loose seat. This meant that they were number four in the suite, and that the chair and loose seat were meant for each other.

The upholstery of these chairs is quite dilapidated, the reason being simply that they have been used, and are in their original Lyons silk covers. The present state of the silk velvet gives no idea how striking the original colouring was, but Arthur pointed out a less faded area of the chair-back from which he had removed the loose seat, to show a much brighter colouring, in green leaves and predominantly red flowers, on a cream background. The effect is brilliant, and shows a little of the kind of impact they must have made when new. But it also opens a debate, which Arthur and Bernard did not have time to go into: what do you do with this suite, which is very important and unique in Britain? Do you keep the original, dilapidated covers, to preserve their historical integrity – or do you restore them to their former splendour by re-covering them? It's a tricky decision to make, between preservation and conservation.

Arthur and Bernard were not able to visit any other rooms in Goodwood on this occasion, although Arthur did see the Dining Room when he came on a different day with chef Michael Smith and they discussed the institution of the 'nineteenth-century English breakfast'.

The Dining Room was much admired by Arthur when he saw it. It forms part of the unfinished Wyatt octagon and is particularly noted for the patterns of its curves, with one side of the room exactly mirroring the other, and for the portraits which hang on the walls: three portraits of the 1st Duke, plus one each of the 1st Duchess, the 2nd Duke and the 2nd Duchess, all painted by Sir Godfrey Kneller. There is also a splendid painting of the 5th Duchess by Sir Thomas Lawrence, which is reputed to have been his favourite among his own works.

Arthur was particularly taken with a late seventeenth-century bracket clock on the mantelpiece, veneered in

would be pleasing and effective, and that the table originally had either a marble or an inlaid top that may at some time have been spoilt, perhaps by water. So perhaps at some later date the plaque was set into the table, replacing the damaged top.

The last furniture that Arthur looked at is in his opinion the *pièce de résistance* of the whole house – a suite of Louis XV furniture comprising one *canapé* (sofa), two *bergères* (wing armchairs), eight *fauteuils à la Reine* (large chairs) and five *fauteuils* (smaller chairs). They boast big moulded giltwood frames, padded arms, carved seat-frames with bold seats, cabriole legs and scroll toes – all in all, big and imposing pieces. As before, Arthur hoped to find a signature, and lifted the chair to find underneath on the

Left *One of the suite of Louis XV furniture by Delanois, in Arthur's opinion the* pièce de résistance *of the whole house. This is a large and impressive armchair, with a big moulded giltwood frame, padded arms, cabriole legs and scroll toes*

Right *The Lyons silk velvet upholstery on the Delanois armchair is original, and still very bright in areas which have been protected from wear and the sun*

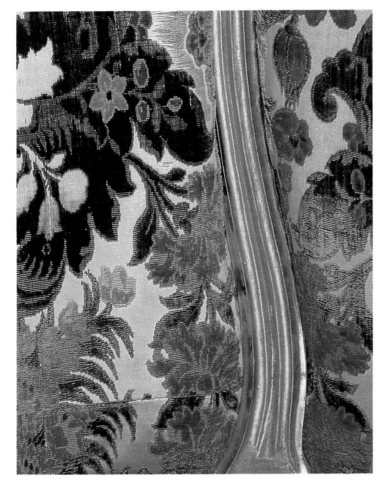

died and completed in 1838 by a local architect. But several pictures do hang here, including one by Van Dyck showing Charles I, Queen Henrietta Maria, Prince Charles and Princess Mary, which belonged to the king until his execution. The remaining pictures include more works by Van Dyck, and some by Kneller and Lely.

The Card Room is reckoned by some to be the loveliest room in the house. It contains three cabinets of Sèvres porcelain, including a pair of *rose pompadour* and apple-green orange-tubs. These are notable in that *rose pompadour* is a very rare colour, discontinued when Madame de Pompadour's patronage ceased, and the only chemist who made the colour died. The room is circular, with a round Axminster carpet as well, and most of the furniture is French, including two delicate inlaid dressing-tables and a Louis XVI *bonheur du jour* or lady's writing-table signed by Feurstein. Its cupboard door is inset with a Sèvres panel showing three exotic birds on a bright green ground – appropriate to a room in which so much porcelain is displayed.

There is more Sèvres porcelain in the alcove of the Yellow Drawing Room, which is the drawing room of the 3rd Duke's great house. Again, it features French furniture, including four Louis XV commodes and two mantel clocks decorated with brass and tortoiseshell marquetry known as Boulle work. Doors lead from here to the main Entrance Hall, the hub of the Wyatt house, which extends the full width of the building. Here hangs a picture of the 5th Duke of Gordon, resplendent in full highland dress, a painting known to millions as the *Cock o' the North*. There are also two views of London by Canaletto. Around 1746-7, many people thought that the man who had just arrived in England claiming to be Canaletto was an impostor (his nephew Bellotto was at the time painting views of Dresden, but trading on his uncle's name). But the 2nd Duke of Richmond, who already had four paintings by the real Canaletto, was not fooled. He let the artist paint views of London from the windows of Richmond House – one showing the Thames and St Paul's, the other depicting Whitehall.

These and the other rooms at Goodwood are well worth visiting for their fine paintings, their furniture and their architecture. Certainly Arthur and Bernard found much to delight them just in the two rooms they looked at in detail; most of all, perhaps, the splendid signed French furniture.

ebony, with an eight-day striking movement and a date recorder. It is a delightful piece, with little ormolu finials above, and the top pierced in basket form, with a carrying handle, but what pleased him most was the maker's name: Johnson, of Chichester. For it must have been brand-new when the 1st Duke bought Goodwood House in 1697, and shows how here, as in other places, the aristocracy supported local industry at the time.

The room has a distinguished history. In 1814 the Tsar of all the Russias dined here, after he came to England following Napoleon's exile to Elba. Edward VII was a frequent visitor, as have been subsequent monarchs, including the Queen, and other members of the Royal Family.

Edward VII was also frequently present at the banquets held in the Ballroom, which used to witness the annual festivities of the July race week. The room was planned by the 3rd Duke to double as a gallery in which to hang the portraits of his royal ancestors. It was unfinished when he

TEMPLE NEWSAM HOUSE

When Arthur Negus visited Temple Newsam House, four miles from the centre of Leeds, with expert in porcelain David Battie, he came expecting 'a most enjoyable time, not so much for architecture as for contents'. Temple Newsam is no longer in private ownership, having been sold in 1922, along with its 917 acres of park, to the city of Leeds by Edward Wood, later Lord Halifax. In this respect the house is the odd one out among those visited by Arthur in this series. Usually he comes to houses still in private hands, and enjoys the feeling that they are loved and lived in. But Temple Newsam makes up for this lack in other ways. Every picture and object in the house is identified and labelled, which makes for a much easier tour, and since the house passed into public ownership the collections have been built up, by gift, bequest and purchase, to add to the paintings and furniture originally left in it, making it a kind of living museum. The collections are also available for study, much as are the objects in any museum, so in a sense they work for their keep.

Arthur's opening remark suggests that the architecture of Temple Newsam House is less than magnificent. A look at the exterior, in comparison with, say, Goodwood, or Wilton House, or Littlecote, will make the point graphically enough. The house dates from the 1520s, and was built by Thomas, Lord Darcy, who inherited in 1488. He constructed a large square building along traditional lines, with an enclosed courtyard, but only the central

Left *The imposing, if not altogether graceful, Elizabethan 'E' plan exterior of Temple Newsam House*

Right *The unusual cluster-column legs that Chippendale incorporated into one of his chairs, found by Arthur in the North-West Room*

Left *The fire-place in the North-West Room. The energy and exuberance of the rococo style are plainly visible not only in the carved pine fire-place, but also in the frame of the picture above it*

block has survived. During the next 100 years it passed out of private ownership twice, anticipating its eventual fate. Lord Darcy became involved in the Pilgrimage of Grace in 1536, an uprising in Yorkshire against Henry VIII which made the mistake of not succeeding. The error was fatal for Darcy, who was duly beheaded for treason, and bad also for Temple Newsam, which was confiscated. Henry VIII then gave the house to the Earl of Lennox, who failed to learn by Darcy's ill luck. He used the house as a centre for political intrigue, one result of which was the marriage of his son, Darnley (who had been born at Temple Newsam), to Mary, Queen of Scots. She was a dangerous lady to be married to, and in 1567 Darnley was murdered – a year after their son, the future James I of England, was born. Queen Elizabeth promptly confiscated Temple Newsam again, but when James I reached the throne he gave it to his cousin, another Duke of Lennox. He couldn't

hold on to it either, being so extravagant that he was forced to sell it for £12,000 to Arthur Ingram, whose family continued to live at Temple Newsam for the next two centuries. Ingram was too smart to be a political agitator. He was a usurer, and by a series of clever and unscrupulous financial deals helped the Stuarts rule without regular grants from Parliament.

Ingram also rebuilt the house, pulling down the east wing and modernising the north and south wings, to create a typical Elizabethan 'E' plan. Externally it has changed little since then. Aesthetically pleasing or not, it is known as the most impressive Tudor-Jacobean house in West Yorkshire.

Arthur and David Battie began in the North-West Room, a corner room on the first floor. It used to be part of the Long Gallery built by Ingram between 1622 and 1636; but a century later the gallery was partitioned so that it no longer ran the entire length of the north wing. As we shall see later, a magnificent remodelled Long Gallery remains, but the partitioning added a library at the north-east end, and a bedchamber at the north-west corner. The North-West Room is 'for a house of this size, a very ordinary small room', as Arthur put it. But it houses some fine English furniture, the first piece to attract their attention being a candlestand, made by Thomas Johnson from one of his own published designs around 1758. (Because Temple Newsam functions as a country house museum, many of its contents are occasionally moved around the house, so the objects mentioned in this visit may no longer be where Arthur and David saw them.) The candlestand delighted both visitors, though David suggested it might benefit from adding a piece of ormolu at the top. It epitomises the rococo style, with fronded 'C' scrolls and two chubby dolphins entwined on the column, and 'an exuberance of acanthus on the base'. It is made entirely from pine, except for iron-cored branches holding the candles with ormolu candle sockets. Rococo was originally French, a reaction against the much heavier baroque style, but Johnson took it to extremes not found in France, and this candlestand is a good example, bursting with energy.

Crossing the room Arthur then stopped at the mantelpiece, contemporary in both date and style. Mid-eighteenth-century mantelpieces were often made of lime or pine, which are, as he observed, good soft woods for a

Left *The mahogany four-kneehole writing-desk, a large and impressive piece based loosely on a published Chippendale design and made for the MP 'Single Speech Hamilton'. Temple Newsam is particularly fortunate in that it also owns another fine library table, designed by Chippendale and originally made for nearby Harewood House*

Above *Cluster columns again: this is how the same Chippendale feature employed on the chairs has been used to very good effect on the four-kneehole writing-desk. The Gothic patterns on the doors are clearly visible as applied fretwork – stuck on, not carved*

Right *The Leeds creamware bust of Minerva. As you can see, the marbled effect of the base is not intended to fool anyone into thinking it's real marble!*

carver to get his tools into. This one is in pine. And the carver has certainly made a thorough job of it – the carving stands right out from the main body of the fire-place. Its colour is not original; at some time in the past it has clearly been stripped and painted, as Arthur noticed. Above it on the wall there hangs a picture in a contemporary frame, which also shows great vitality and movement, important elements of the rococo style. It features exaggerated 'C' scrolls, with pendants of fruit and flowers, 'dribbling down', in a manner that reminded Arthur of Grinling Gibbons.

He moved on to furniture of a rather different type: a pair of Chippendale chairs. The contrast in style between the exuberance of the mantelpiece and candlestand and the formal restraint of the chairs led David to query the date,

but Arthur confirmed them as within a year or two of 1760, so all are contemporary with each other. They display Gothic influence in their upright slats, but also boast one unusual feature, raised as they are on turned columns known as 'cluster-column legs'. These rare cluster columns recur in the adjacent mahogany four knee-hole library writing-desk of the same date. The doors on the desk carry a Gothic pattern which is different from the rococo style not only in look but in method: instead of the rococo carving the patterns here are carried out in applied fretwork – stuck on, rather than pierced. The design is loosely based on an illustration in Chippendale's *The Gentleman and Cabinet Maker's Director*, first published in 1754, and comprising sample drawings for furniture that were widely admired and copied. It became tremendously influential during the eighteenth century, containing as it did 160 line engravings of very fine designs, so that, despite it costing three and a half guineas to buy, many furniture-makers made sure they had a copy. It ran into several editions, and abridged copies of it can still be purchased today.

One of the great features of Temple Newsam, as both Arthur and David observed, is that a lot is known about many of the objects there, and a large amount of documentation concerning them still survives. The table which Arthur and David were examining, however, has no need of separate documentation: there is a brass plate on its top, which reads: 'William Gerard Hamilton, known as "Single Speech Hamilton", MP for 42 years, Born 28 January 1729, Died 16 July 1796'. This table was known to have been made for the house by the Earl and Countess of Pomfret of Arlington Street, London, where Hamilton resided after the Countess's death. Though nicknamed 'Single Speech', and though Arthur and David joked about the extraordinary prospect of a man who was an MP for forty-two years making only one speech in all that time, it is known that this epithet was unjustly earned. Hamilton gained the tag following his maiden speech to Parliament on 13 November 1755, after he had been an MP for seven months. It lasted from two o'clock in the afternoon to a quarter to five the next morning! No report of the speech exists, though Horace Walpole wrote that 'his figure is advantageous, his voice strong and clear, his manner spirited, and the whole with the ease of an established speaker'; Walpole went on to extol the talents of this 'young Mr Hamilton, who spoke for the first time and was at once perfection', by comparing him favourably with no less a speaker than Pitt. Hamilton went on to make a number of speeches in the house, leading to his being appointed Chancellor of the Exchequer in Ireland in 1763. He maintained his reputation for brilliant oratory for the rest of his life, though nothing survives for us to judge. The last word on him should rest with a lady – the diarist Fanny Burney: 'This Mr Hamilton is extremely tall and handsome, has an air of haughty and fashionable superiority, is intelligent, dry, sarcastic and clever. I should have received much pleasure from his conversational powers had I not previously been prejudiced against him by hearing that he is infinitely artful, double, and crafty.'

Clearly the writing-desk at Temple Newsam dates from the time when he was at the height of his popularity as a persuasive young orator; it was executed in a fashionable new style, if not by Chippendale himself then by an equally good imitator. And, as if to show how universally Chippendale's designs spread, upon the desk David found a pair of silver candlesticks whose design had clearly been borrowed from the *Director*. They have cluster-column stems, just like the chair and writing-desk and, as David noticed, even the tracery at the foot of the sticks has the same Gothic pattern as the desk. Each candlestick carries the hallmark for 1765, and their unity of style with the desk further underlines these two fashions of the mid-eighteenth century: the French rococo as against the restrained Gothic motifs that bespeak a particularly English style. One of the richnesses of Temple Newsam is its variety of treasures spanning a multitude of styles over several centuries.

Although David and Arthur were not able to pursue this theme throughout the house, and no complete interiors from the early sixteenth century survive, many of the major decorative styles from then until Victorian times are on display. The Bretton Room, for instance, features late Gothic linenfold panelling and sixteenth-century furniture; throughout the house there is much silver and porcelain of the seventeenth century, as well as a Stuart day bed and companion settees which are majestic and luxurious, reflecting continental ideas of taste. The Library is a beautiful example of the Palladian style of the early eighteenth century, a form of classicism inspired by Lord

Right *The portrait in the North-West Room of Henry, 7th Viscount, and Lady Irwin, painted by Philip Mercier. Temple Newsam House stands in the background, and the scroll proudly held by the viscount shows a sketch for a ceiling roundel in the Long Gallery*

Left *A detail of the salt-glazed stoneware bowl, decorated with Chinese scenes*

ANNE HIS WIFE, DAUGHTER
To CHARLES SCARBOROUGH, Esqr.
HENRY INGRAM THE SEVENTH
VISCOUNT IRWIN.

colourfully imitates the appearance of marble, though as David pointed out, no marble ever looked quite like that.

Not to be outdone by the silver candlestick that echoes a motif from the Chippendale-style library writing-desk, David now came upon a piece of agate ware the same shape as a silver jug. 'In my field, ceramics, the porcelain-makers nearly always copied the silversmiths' – who, it seems, sometimes copied the cabinet-makers. Arthur identified the silver jug as a George II piece, around 1740. The agate ware copy dates from about twenty years later. It is, for all that, a colourful and attractive piece; in agate ware, the design runs all the way through the pottery: what they did was to take the different coloured clays, mix them together, and then pot them.

The house has other agate ware and David stopped to admire a teapot, moulded with a scallop shell pattern. He then came upon another teapot, also moulded with scallop shells. One of the joys of Temple Newsam's huge ceramics collections is that within its variety there occur many similarities and opportunities for comparison. This second teapot is in salt-glazed stoneware, and decorated in brilliant *famille rose* enamel painting, of a jewel-like quality that David likened to a stained-glass window. But when David picked up another piece of salt-glazed stoneware, a large bowl painted with Chinese scenes, it was Arthur's turn to be surprised. It features a very rare subject for decoration, a lady and gentleman taking wine round a table, but as Arthur immediately noticed, the table is out of all proportion. In a real table of the period, the spread of the legs should almost equal the width of the top. In this decorated scene, the legs are only about half wide enough. The same oddity occurs with the wineglasses from which they are drinking: the foot of each glass is tiny compared with the bowl, whereas it should be of equal or greater width. At least the artist got one thing right: the lady and gentleman are holding their glasses by the foot, not by the stem, which was how a glass was normally held in those days.

These are just a few of the items that attracted David Battie's attention amid a huge number that Arthur and he did not have time to look at. The Oak Cabinet Room, for instance, is full of Chinese blue-and-white porcelain of the eighteenth century. There is also much English ware, including Staffordshire, Chelsea, Derby and Wedgwood, as well, of course, as Leeds.

Burlington and William Kent. Historically this was followed by the rococo and Gothic Revival styles which Arthur and David had been considering, and then by neoclassicism, pioneered by Robert Adam in particular. Thomas Chippendale in fact made another writing-table in the neoclassical style during 1770, or thereabouts, which is now at Temple Newsam, and is one of the most celebrated pieces of furniture there.

The advent of mass-production methods in the eighteenth century led to the fame of Leeds pottery, many examples of which can be seen around the house. Temple Newsam has one of the finest collections of Leeds ware in the country and some good examples can be seen in the Hollings bequest. But it was a pair of rococo dolphins that first caught David Battie's specialist eye. They are typical of the style, with a shell base and other motifs reminiscent of the mantelpiece and picture-frame Arthur had already stopped to admire. On this occasion the dolphins were placed on that mantelpiece, either side of a bust of Minerva, goddess of war, also in Leeds creamware of the period but, unlike the dolphins, brilliantly painted. Arthur was particularly taken by the base of the little bust, which

Above *One of the roundels in the Long Gallery ceiling. This one contains a sculpted portrait of King George I; others feature similar representations of other members of the royal family*

From looking at the porcelain laid out in the North-West Room, Arthur raised his eyes to see a portrait of Henry, 7th Viscount, and Lady Irwin, by Philip Mercier. The Viscount is appropriately holding a scroll on which is a sketch of one of the ceiling roundels from the adjacent Long Gallery; for he it was who, between 1738 and 1745, remodelled this wing of Temple Newsam, partitioning the old Long Gallery. Arthur's point in mentioning him was that the 7th Viscount was responsible for many of the furnishings of the house, as well as for much of the decoration.

And the decoration in the Long Gallery, which they now entered, is certainly impressive. Arthur noted that it's

something of an undertaking to turn a bare Long Gallery of the early seventeenth century into a smaller, more 'modern' and attractive saloon. The ceiling is one of the most striking features, magnificently executed by Thomas Perritt and Joseph Rose of York; their ceilings certainly did not fall down, as James Wyatt's did at Wilton! The original receipts for the work survive and the total bill for the ceiling at the time came to less than £200. As David remarked, it had just been restored, at a price which adds several noughts onto the original cost. The ceiling is largely comprised of roundels such as that depicted in the painting of the 7th Viscount. In several roundels portraits of royalty and nobility are sculpted. One of them features

Left *The Long Gallery: a colourful and attractive saloon, created by the 7th Viscount by shortening the bare earlier Long Gallery. The magnificent ceiling has recently been restored*

Right *One of the girandoles in the Long Gallery – an extravagant and lively example of the rococo style, by James Pascall. In the lower half of the candle bracket a hound chases a stag diagonally left to right*

George I, another represents George II, and others show his children, daughter-in-law and grandchildren. In all, the bill charges for '13 medals at 10s. 6d. each', which was a fairly standard price for such work at the time.

Looking round the room, Arthur speculated that rooms on this scale were designed more for show than for living in. Even though as a saloon it is shorter than the original, it is still splendid and grand. Arthur led David to one of the girandoles or candle brackets on the wall. Its size and extravagance of style would be overpowering in any smaller room, but it fits in perfectly here. It was thought to have been made by Matthias Lock until a letter was found from one James Pascall, enclosing an account for

'two rich girandoles with two branches and six lights, gilt, in burnished gold, £50'. Pascall is not a well-known figure, but his work here is excellent English rococo, with bulrushes, a hound chasing a stag, and everything bursting in lively profusion.

Next to it is a tall mirror, over 8 feet high. Arthur described it as transitional in style, with a reminder of William Kent in the mask head on top, while the two exotic birds alighting on the mirror are more like Chippendale in style. There is a branch design which curls in and out around the frame, making the whole piece rich and impressive. It is made of two glass plates, because the methods at the time – blowing the glass, opening it out

Above *A settee and two of the chairs from the large suite by James Pascall, in the Long Gallery. Rococo furniture, but the upholstery coverings provided by the ladies of the house are more reminiscent of seventeenth-century Dutch designs*

Left *One of the biscuit porcelain parrots in the Long Gallery, with ormolu mounts by Henri Dasson. Though it seems to fit well with the rococo style of the room, it in fact dates from the late nineteenth century*

'stuffed in the white', which indicates that no upholstery coverings were yet put on them. These would have been added by the ladies of the house and, as Arthur mentioned, by professional embroiderers as well. Although the design of the furniture itself is rococo, the upholstery, painstakingly executed in gros-point needlework, harks back to the Dutch flower pieces of the previous century in its rather less flamboyant pattern.

It is a splendid suite in a magnificent room, but David and Arthur, to their regret, had no time left to look further. There are, however, several other rooms that warrant visiting, one or two of which should be briefly mentioned here.

The south wing was converted in 1796, creating upstairs a spacious suite of bed and dressing rooms. This made for several noteworthy features, including an elegant stone staircase with a fine wrought-iron balustrade and cast-brass ornament in the north-west stairwell. The Great Hall features a dignified neoclassical chimney-piece, and the Chinese Drawing Room boasts hand-painted Chinese wallpaper added in the 1820s. In Victorian times, more additions in the form of deal panelling and plaster ornaments were superimposed on most of the features added to the Great Hall in 1796, and an impressive oak staircase, one of the most attractive features in the entire house, was also put in. The owner at the time, Mrs Meynell-Ingram, wanted to recapture the past in her modernisations; thus the staircase was based on a genuine Elizabethan one from Slaugham Place, Sussex, and the Darnley Room and the corridor on the first floor of the west wing were decorated in pseudo-Jacobean style.

Alterations were made in the park also, which had been redesigned in the 1760s by 'Capability' Brown, but the east prospect, with its temple and distant vista, still reflects his ideas. Nowadays the kitchen garden houses a dazzling display of roses and glasshouse plants, and the park has become known for its spectacular show of rhododendrons and azaleas.

So the park and the house, spanning the centuries from Tudor to Victorian times, well repay a visit, although Arthur and David Battie came primarily to look at the contents, especially the rococo furniture and fine porcelain, with the wealth of documentary evidence about them which survives. Living museum rather than family home it may be, but it is a fascinating house none the less.

flat, and then floating the silver onto the back – could not accommodate large enough pieces of glass to make the whole mirror in one plate.

Under the mirror, on the table, were some pieces that interested David, largely because he disagreed with the existing descriptions of them. They are two Chinese ormolu-mounted porcelain parrots, and, in David's words, 'absolutely fitting with the style of the room, and for long believed to be contemporary – even in the books as such. But if we look at the back, engraved into the ormolu: Henri Dasson 1887.' So the signature gives it away – not mid-eighteenth-century at all, but brilliant nineteenth-century reproductions. It is curious that the signature went unnoticed for so long. David described Dasson as probably the best ormolu-maker of the period, which may be part of the reason why the imitation is so convincing. In between the parrots stands a Chinese vase. It was also believed to be eighteenth-century, but as David pointed out, the Chinese did not make vases with the sort of bronze bands that can be seen on the vase until the 1880s. He considered its ormolu mounts also to be 'pure Victorian revival'.

Finally Arthur looked at a suite, again made by James Pascall and comprising twenty chairs, four settees and a day bed. The Pascall letter contains his account for this too: the chairs cost two and a half guineas each, and the day bed seven guineas. The bill describes the suite as

LUTON HOO

Arthur's visit to Luton Hoo in Bedfordshire was in some ways an especial pleasure: for he brought as guest his friend Hermione Waterfield, a respected expert from a major auction house, to see in particular a collection of objects by a maker of whom she is extremely fond – Carl Fabergé. Luton Hoo contains the finest collection of Fabergé (apart from the royal family's) in the country, as well as a large number of other important treasures. The house is imbued with grandeur, as Hermione observed as they entered the Pillared Hall – there is a splendid lingering atmosphere. But as Arthur replied, there have been some devastating fires here, and the Hall is not original to the house.

The site of Luton Hoo may have been occupied since prehistoric times – the word 'Hoo' means the spur of a hill in Old Saxon – and it is apparently a likely site for a pagan grove. Certainly Roman coins and remains have been found close by. It is known that from the thirteenth century at least there was a manor-house here, which was owned by a variety of families, mostly not of great note, until it was sold in 1762 for £94,700 to John Stuart, 3rd Earl of Bute.

Bute had become Prime Minister in 1760 and by 1763 he was sufficiently unpopular to lose his job. He may have been no one's idea of a statesman, but he knew enough to hire Robert Adam, the great architect whose name recurs throughout this book, to build him a new house, expense no object. Work began in 1767, but then came the first fire in 1771. Undeterred, they tried again, and about half of Adam's plans came to fruition. In particular, the 146-foot-long Library was a masterpiece; even Adam was pleased enough to call it his 'chef-d'oeuvre both in point of elegance and contrivance'. Many considered it second only to Blenheim. And while Adam was at work inside, 'Capability' Brown was busy at a bit of landscape gardening, extending the small park of 300 acres to 1,200, damming

Left *The entrance front of Luton Hoo. Sir Robert Smirke erected the portico when he completed this front in about 1830. It was shored up after the disastrous fire of 1843*

95

Right *The Pillared Hall, which was rebuilt with pillars once Sir Julius Wernher bought Luton Hoo in 1903, and then became the main salon for entertaining. It was refurbished with panelling after the Second World War, when Sir Harold and Lady Zia Wernher took possession of the house again*

the river Lea in two places, and constructing two lakes.

We shall never know for sure how wonderful all this looked. The park was altered in Victorian times, and Bute's great-grandson, when he took over the property in 1814, employed Sir Robert Smirke to make extensive alterations, including some to the façade. If that wasn't enough, in 1843 came another fire, which destroyed nearly everything. Some pictures and part of the Library were saved but the flames accounted for the rest. The house was rebuilt some years later, though the façade was not altered much at this time. It wasn't until 1903, when Sir Julius Wernher bought it, that the house's transition to its current architectural form began. The Pillared Hall, for example, was rebuilt to become the main salon for entertaining; it still performs this function today.

Sir Julius was a great collector, as was his wife, who remarried after his death to become Lady Ludlow. It was by the portrait of her in the Pillared Hall that Arthur and Hermione first paused. Arthur noted that the house contains a splendid collection of English porcelain, which Lady Ludlow built up and which is named after her. Unfortunately, there was no time during this visit to see it. It is exhibited in three rooms opening from the Upper Corridor. The first room contains Chelsea and Bow, including a Chelsea part tea service with Chinese figures, which has been described as 'among England's finest porcelain accomplishments'. The second room is devoted to Worcester, the only eighteenth-century English porcelain factory to have survived down to the present day. The final room contains pieces from a number of factories, including Derby, Plymouth and Bristol, and nineteenth-century porcelain from, among others, Spode, Swansea and the Staffordshire factories. It is a fine collection, which no visitor should ignore. Arthur and Hermione, however, with very limited time, were committed to viewing other objects.

Without further ado, Hermione picked up a dish by Fabergé – as she noted, this was Lady Ludlow's contribution to that collection. It was made from one solid piece of nephrite – Russian jade – with gold handles decorated in French eighteenth-century taste, incorporating translucent strawberry enamel, and rose diamonds. On the back it is quite plain; after all, if nobody was going to look at it, why should Fabergé waste time on decoration? It is in any case one of the largest pieces he made – he usually worked

Left *The cigarette box by Carl Fabergé that was said to have been presented to the tsar in 1913, as one of many pieces Fabergé made to celebrate the tercentenary of the Romanov dynasty. The Russian eagle here frames portraits of Tsar Nicholas II and Tsarina Alexandra Feodorovna*

Right *The unusual mahogany globe, which opens out to reveal itself as a bureau. It dates from about 1810, and incorporates a band of ebony inlay that confirms that it was made after the death of Nelson*

on a much smaller scale – and measures 17½ inches in length, with a tray diameter of 10 inches.

Next to it had been placed a cigarette box by the same maker. It is made of gold, encrusted with diamonds, and decorated with translucent green enamel. In the centre, framed by a Russian eagle in diamonds, are small portraits of Tsar Nicholas II and Tsarina Alexandra Feodorovna. Fabergé probably made it to celebrate the tercentenary of the Romanov dynasty in 1913. Despite the date, it employs Napoleonic motifs, and Hermione described it as in simple taste.

Arthur agreed that he both liked and admired the box, but expressed strong reservations about two photograph frames next to it on the table. As he said, this is where personal taste comes in – the frames left him cold, despite the fact that they were probably by Fabergé. Hermione could not let this go without comment. As she pointed out, they are simple things, such as the very rich often like. And though they are only made of wood and silver, who but Fabergé could achieve the crisp folding of the silver into the appearance of a ribbon and bow, imitating the

effect of satin? Impressive as they were to Hermione, Arthur could still take them or leave them.

But when they crossed the length of the Pillared Hall, Arthur came across an item that interested him enormously. It is a mahogany globe with its stand, made in segments and then veneered – a most unusual-looking piece. When closed, it hides its real secret; for it opens in such a way that two of the quadrants forming the upper hemisphere fold back outwards – revealing that it is really a bureau. There are drawers in both the doors and the back, which are very neat and make the piece unique as far as we know. Arthur mentioned that a similar globe exists, but it opens into a work-table rather than a bureau. This one was made by Morgan and Saunders, a firm which also supplied furniture to Nelson's cabin on board the *Victory*; Arthur dated it to around 1810. The whole nation went into mourning on Nelson's death in 1805 – and furniture was put into mourning too. There is a band of black inlay around the rim of the globe and, as Arthur noted, it was at this Regency period that such a colour inlay was re-introduced. Taking a drawer out, he then showed the

joints to Hermione – they have miniature dovetails which fit together perfectly, so that you couldn't break them if you tried. The beautiful cedar drawers smelt just like new to him.

The globe bureau was one of the pieces that Sir Julius Wernher's son, Sir Harold, added to the house when he came into possession of it in 1945. He had noted the lack of good English furniture, and acted to rectify it. He also further enriched the collection of Dutch paintings. In 1917 Sir Harold had married Lady Anastasia (Zia) Mikhailovna Torby, elder daughter of the Grand Duke Michael of Russia and the Countess de Torby. The Grand Duke was a grandson of Tsar Nicholas I, and great-great-grandson of Catherine the Great. The Countess de Torby's grandfather was Alexander Pushkin, the Russian poet, which means that Lady Zia had as great-grandparents both Pushkin and Nicholas I – a relationship that would have horrified both ancestors!

When Sir Harold and Lady Zia made Luton Hoo their home again after 1945 (the house had been used as the Headquarters of Eastern Command during the Second World War), they refurbished the Pillared Hall with panelling, and decided initially to open the greater part of their art collection to visitors. Since then, more of the house has been opened.

The collection of Fabergé was mainly inherited by Lady Zia from her parents. One exception is the presentation cigarette box, which was a gift to Lady Zia from her husband.

And it was to more pieces by Fabergé laid out on a cabinet that Arthur and Hermione now progressed. Here was a group of more practical items, for everyday use. Hermione particularly liked a little blotter in the form of a small roller. It is a purely utilitarian object, but made special by the silver-gilt in the frame, exquisitely patterned in little leaves, and by the moonstones at the foot and in the handle, with pink enamel on the handle to set the whole thing off. It is a very well-made piece, with a light touch. This lightness in fact characterises the other objects on display on the cabinet. There was a delightful bell-push in pink and white enamels, and some little taper sticks in deep blue and yellow, the racing colours of the Rothschild

family, who probably commissioned them. On their bases are neat bands of foliage in one colour of gold, finished with a darker gold band. As Hermione commented, everything is very succinct – tasteful but uncomplicated.

Arthur was impressed, but no less so by the cabinet upon which these items were displayed. For it is an extremely rare piece made by a *maître ébéniste* called Jean-François Oeben, whom Arthur described as one of the finest French cabinet-makers who ever lived. He preferred mechanical items, specialising in the compact, elaborately fitted, multi-purpose pieces which came into demand during the second half of the eighteenth century in France, with the new fashion for smaller and more intimate rooms such as boudoirs. This cabinet has, as Arthur observed, one or two tricks up its sleeve. The front seems to be a lovely set of drawers in tulipwood and kingwood, both types of rosewood; but the top two drawers fold down as a flap. From here Arthur picked out a key which he inserted in the side of the cabinet, and

began to wind: and lo and behold, up rose a fitment at the back. This too is magnificent – huge panels of tulipwood with kingwood, lovely ormolu mounts and a pretty catch which turns out to release the front panel. This drops down to reveal bookshelves; so it is a delightful cabinet with bookshelves on top. But press another catch, this time at the fitment corner, and the sides spin round to show off little blue-lined pockets containing utensils in glass, porcelain and silver-gilt for eating and drinking. It is remarkable to what lengths a cabinet-maker would go to ensure that a lady had everything – and he still hadn't finished. One of the drawers is fitted out with a little writing-slide, and lower down was a prie-dieu (now a drawer), for kneeling to pray on. Altogether this one piece of furniture seems to include all the items a lady would need. It is a delightful and quite remarkable item, properly known as a *table à la bourgogne*.

From one fine piece of furniture to another, this time English – a three chair-back settee. As Arthur pointed out,

Left *Everyday items by Fabergé: on the left, the little blotter, in the centre two tiny taper sticks in blue and yellow, the racing colours of the Rothschild family, and on the right the bell-push in pink and white enamels*

Right *The* table à la bourgogne *by the maître ébéniste Jean-François Oeben. The top two drawers have folded down as a flap, the bookshelves have risen at the top, and the sides are open to display its blue-lined pockets*

it was given its name for an obvious reason – the back is shaped like three chairs. It has good pierced and carved upright splats or centre panels, and is of a Gothic design, dating from around 1760. Arthur admired its beautifully shaped and carved arms and its very unusual square taper legs. Almost every part of the settee is carved, including the prettily shaped understretcher. It is clearly Chippendale, and has a fine needlework seat with a large central panel in petit-point and a wide outer border in gros-point. But what fascinated Arthur most was the fact that the Victoria and Albert Museum has a pair of matching armchairs. So what happened to disperse the suite and, more particularly, what became of the rest of the chairs that there must have been?

After the disastrous conflagration of 1843, Luton Hoo was sold to one John Shaw Leigh, a rich solicitor from Liverpool, who set about rebuilding the house, without seriously altering the façade, which had been shored up since the fire. His daughter-in-law then inherited and she married the Danish Ambassador to England. Madame de Falbe was apparently a lady of eccentricities 'long remembered in the neighbourhood of Luton'. It was when she died in 1903 that Sir Julius Wernher purchased the house. Apart from his wife's porcelain, Sir Julius himself was a most noteworthy collector and he built up a very fine art collection, much of which can be seen in the Main Gallery. Many of the pictures are on religious themes, including works by Filippino Lippi, Memlinc and Bermejo. One of the house's finest paintings, Altdorfer's masterpiece, *Christ Taking Leave of his Mother before the Passion*, was sold in 1980 to the National Gallery for what was believed to be the highest figure ever paid for a single painting, in any country. In 1885 it fetched no more than twenty-three guineas at Christie's; times certainly change! This recent sale was forced upon the trustees of the Wernher Collection following the death of Lady Zia in 1977 – a harsh reminder of the economic realities involved in maintaining and endowing a house and collection today.

Sir Julius collected other superb objects – medieval ivories, Renaissance jewels and bronzes, German silver-gilt, Limoges enamels and Italian glazed pottery known as maiolica. They are outstanding in both number and quality but, like the porcelain collection, could not be seen by Arthur and Hermione on this occasion. They did have time, however, to see more of Lady Zia's contribution to

Luton Hoo – those marvellous pieces by Fabergé.

Hermione sat at a table upon which were set out several small items. The first she looked at was a remarkable spray of the plant gypsophila, very thin, very fragile, and with very delicate tracery. The gold stalk has a number of soldered off-shoots, set with tiny diamonds; to Hermione it's one of the loveliest pieces Fabergé ever made. And this slender, naturalistic *tour de force* sits in a plain, almost squat, vase of green nephrite. Arthur described it as 'ordinary', which Hermione agreed with, noting that much of what Fabergé created was indeed in a sense ordinary. For instance, he designed all manner of little animals, only a couple of inches long. His modellers would craft them first in wax, then he would have them cut in different-coloured stones. Lady Zia's mother, the Countess de Torby, was particularly fond of elephants; two models were in front of Hermione, one grey, the other pink. Many of the animals – a proud cockerel, for example – were made in green nephrite. Some have specific functions, such as a fish that doubles as an electric bell-push, and a frog parasol handle. Others seem to contain caricatures of Fabergé's clients. A walrus, for instance, was no doubt meant to represent a rather bluff colonel. It is extremely expressive, capturing in stone the folds of the flesh as they fall over the bones, and telling a whole story just in the way it sits. As Hermione noted, only Fabergé captured the essence of the whole animal in his models, yet he never physically made anything himself. However, he would not accept less than the very best from his workmasters; no blemish was permitted to mar the perfection he demanded. It is said that he kept by him a steel dish and a hammer. If anything came to him flawed, he lifted the hammer and smashed the offending object to smithereens!

Arthur asked who Fabergé was. Born in St Petersburg in 1846 of Huguenot descent, he was educated in Dresden, Italy, France and England; so when he and his brother inherited their father's jewellery establishment in 1870, he had already seen something of the world. As Hermione recounted, his workshop soon acquired fame for its objects of fantasy – exquisite masterpieces such as flowers, figure groups and animals. His emphasis was less on splendour than on design, fine craftsmanship and the best materials. He became jeweller to Alexander III and Nicholas II, the last two tsars of Russia, from 1881 to

Right *Small animals by Fabergé. The fish on the left is an electric bell-push, and the frog on the right doubles as a parasol handle. Hermione particularly liked the way the folds of flesh fall over the bones of the walrus. You can see why she guessed that it was based on a bluff colonel!*

Left *One of Fabergé's flower sprays, only a few inches high. This one is gypsophila, and comprises a gold stalk with a number of soldered off-shoots, set with little diamonds, growing out of a nephrite vase*

1917, and his finest work was largely the tiny gold, enamelled and jewelled objects he made for the Russian imperial family and their friends. In 1884 Alexander commissioned for his tsarina the first of Fabergé's celebrated imperial Easter eggs, which soon became the delight of European and Asian royalty alike. Nicholas II took a personal interest in the production of these eggs, which contained 'surprise' presents for the tsarina and for his mother, the dowager empress, each year.

But Fabergé made Easter eggs for the less exclusive sections of the market as well. After all, as Hermione explained, an Easter egg was a particularly useful gift: it

was about the only present a gentlemen could give a lady without compromising her reputation – anything else, and a girl's parents would frown on her. Fabergé used to present them on heart-shaped trays, each at different prices. A string of them was displayed on the table in front of Hermione.

Next to it was a small heart in pink enamel, blue enamel and gold, with a picture inside and the names 'Nadejda' engraved on the back and 'Zia' on the front, both encrusted with diamonds. Hermione was particularly impressed by this piece, because enamelling takes such an enormously long time. Layer after layer has to be applied, each one having to be buffed down smooth before the next can go on; and then the pins to hold the diamonds have to be drilled through the enamel in cold water, to prevent the heat generated by the drilling from shattering the enamel.

Alongside it on the table was a seventh anniversary present in pink enamel for Lady Zia's parents, Grand Duke Michael and the Countess de Torby. It features the years 1891 and 1898 – the period of their marriage at that time – and also the figure 'II', to represent the month of February. For the day of the month it offers '14/26' – two different

days, because at that time there was a twelve-day difference between the Russian calendar and the one used in Britain.

And looking at other items on the table, it was clear how wide Fabergé's appeal was. He could work with equal facility in any of a range of styles, from splendid imperial pieces to simple designs for the wealthier echelons of ordinary society. A delightful round pin comprising a green circle with a flower was made in the art nouveau style with which he was completely at home; so was a triangular moss agate brooch. Both pieces were intended for the cheaper end of the market, yet perfect in their way.

The final piece of Fabergé Hermione looked at was a forget-me-not spray set in rock crystal hollowed out so as to appear to be water in a vase. Flower sprays like this were also made by rivals – Cartier, for instance – and the hardstones used would have been fairly easy to set. It is occasionally difficult at first to be certain who the maker was. But it was Fabergé who best achieved the natural twist of the stems, the almost organic imitation of the manner of their growth. He could capture the natural and supply the very rich with a simple object for their amusement, or he could equally well provide an extravagant and showy piece when asked.

Fabergé's work came to an end with the Russian Revolution. It had been slowing down anyway during the First World War, as funds were recalled and his workmen were called up to fight. He eventually left Russia as courier to the British Embassy – he had always had strong links with England. His only shop outside Russia was in Dover Street in London, and later in Bond Street. But it was to Switzerland that he went to live, and he was buried at Cannes, under a large porphyry slab. As Arthur agreed, he was a quite fantastic jeweller.

As if to emphasise the skill and delicacy of his work, Arthur and Hermione looked at some pieces from two chess sets made in Jagpur, in enamelled gold. The enamelling on these Indian chessmen is thick and slabby, and probably would have found no favour with Fabergé. The pieces have colour, dash and showmanship, but not the delicacy and attention to detail he always required.

And there, for reasons of time, the visit – not only to the house, but to the work and story of Fabergé – had to come to an end. When Arthur thanked his guest for having accompanied him, one might have detected an extra warmth in appreciation of the way she brought to life the work of the great jeweller with whom so much of their visit was concerned.

There is, of course, much more to see at Luton Hoo, particularly the other collections that were built up by Sir Julius Wernher, Lady Ludlow and Lady Zia Wernher. It is sadly not possible to do real justice to any of them here, noteworthy as they are both in quality and quantity.

The Dutch Room, for instance, is primarily given over to seventeenth-century Dutch pictures with works by, among others, Rembrandt, Frans Hals, van der Heyden and van der Velde the younger. A large number of other paintings, along with the Renaissance jewellery and Italian maiolica, are to be found in the Main Gallery. In the Ivory Room can be seen a collection of ivory which, like the Renaissance jewels, is one of the most important private collections in Britain. The subject matter of the ivories is mostly religious, from Byzantine work of the tenth century to French examples from 400 years later. Also on display are two wings from a rare English ivory triptych; the centre plaque can be seen in the Victoria and Albert Museum. It seems that it was, regrettably, a common practice for this kind of item to be divided between collectors in the nineteenth century. Nowadays it seems a quite shameful thing to do.

Other collections are also on display. The Upper Corridor, for instance, houses German silver-gilt from the sixteenth and seventeenth centuries, while the Lower Corridor, along with its excellent English furniture, boasts a large collection of French Limoges enamels, mainly from the same period as the silver-gilt. And just off this corridor is the Brown Jack Room, so called after Sir Harold Wernher's racehorse which was one of the finest in racing history. The room is devoted to the sport, and features a number of pictures of racehorses, some very successful and famous, owned by Sir Harold and Lady Zia.

Other rooms are worth a visit not so much for the objects they contain as for their decoration. The Blue Hall in the centre of the house, for instance, boasts a number of French tapestries; those on the walls were woven at the Gobelins factory in the early eighteenth century. Below one of them stands a suite of eight armchairs and a sofa, covered in Beauvais tapestry and dating from around 1780. The Dining Room features on the wall a set of Beauvais tapestries depicting 'The Story of the King of China'. They are remarkably bright, due to the fact that they were rolled up for many years. The dining-table is laid for dessert, with the side-tables set with silver-gilt. Much of this, as well as the cut glass, can claim royal connections – mostly through the Duke of Cumberland, King George III's son, who became King of Hanover in 1837 when Queen Victoria was prevented by law from succeeding to the Hanoverian throne.

The French decoration in these two rooms and in the Marble Hall and Grand Stairs, which are themselves impressive items of French workmanship, was introduced by Sir Julius. As we have noticed, it is he whom we chiefly have to thank for the current good health of Luton Hoo, for his attention to the house and his collecting. But on Arthur and Hermione's visit the collection provided by his daughter-in-law, Lady Zia, was the centre of attention. Apart from the works by Fabergé, the Russian Rooms also house portraits, photographs and personal possessions (including a silver trophy and travelling dessert service, and three striking court dresses), that all belonged to a branch of the Romanovs, the Russian imperial family. All in all there is much to see and to admire.

Right *The Fabergé heart in pink and blue enamel and gold, with the names 'Nadejda' and 'Zia' encrusted with diamonds. Under it sits the seventh anniversary brooch for Grand Duke Michael and the Countess of Torby*

KINGSTONE LISLE PARK

The house and park of Kingstone Lisle lie near Wantage on the northern edge of the Berkshire Downs, in rolling countryside. Seen from across the park, the house sits in an elegant and stately fashion amid its dramatic parkland – a magnificent view that one would have expected to have been a ready subject for late eighteenth- and early nineteenth-century engravers. But no such views seem to have been published; as Marcus Binney noted in *Country Life*, 'It is almost as if a conspiracy of silence has been drawn over it.'

Here Arthur brought a friend of many years' standing, Robin Butler, who in Arthur's words 'has written a book on English furniture which I consider one of the best I've ever read'. They began their visit in the Entrance Hall, which dates from the nineteenth century – but the estate itself is much older.

In the Middle Ages it belonged to the de Lisle family, from whom it takes its name. In 1336 Alice de Lisle imparked 200 acres, so the estate must date from this time. The Hyde family bought the manor in 1538, though they did not move until 1617: but no trace survives of a house of this date, for it was burned down. The central part of the present house was built in 1677: a stone beneath the garden front was revealed some years ago, bearing this date. Between 1818 and 1820 the house was considerably altered, and two wings were added on the north side. By this time the house was in another family's hands, having been sold in 1749 to one Abraham Atkins, 'a successful speculator in the South Sea Scheme' and 'a Presbyterian [who] gave divers lands, etc., for the benefit of dissenting congregations in various counties; among them Kingstone Lisle'. His son's nephew's son commissioned the addition

Left *Kingstone Lisle in its delightful setting, seen from across the parkland. Though the central part of the house was built in 1677, it was considerably altered between 1818 and 1820*

109

Left *The bureau bookcase in the Hall, with its candle-slides that still retain their candlesticks. The piece is a fine example of its kind, in figured walnut, dating from around 1715*
Right *One of the candlesticks from the bureau bookcase. It is just possible to make out the vertical seam running up it, that reveals its method of construction and confirms its date, which the hallmark indicates as 1740*

out on display and in use as a container for logs in the Hall.

Near it Arthur came upon a late eighteenth-century oval open wine cooler. He remarked that these days you usually find such things hidden away under a sideboard because people don't know what to do with them. There is no longer much practical use for what is basically a wide, shallow wooden bucket; refrigerators have made them obsolete. So when he saw this one in the Hall with flowers in it, doubling as a *jardinière*, he was particularly intrigued. Robin suggested that period wine coolers may have been made with this second purpose in mind. Certainly, they do the job well enough.

A few paces down the Hall was a globe-stand, but with a bowl featuring a pretty floral pattern sitting in it. The globes that went with such stands would have been made of papier mâché, and tended to disintegrate easily; so it is quite common for a stand to survive, but not its globe. Again, instead of being consigned to the attic the stand has been put to use here. And Robin was quite taken with it, dating it from the beginning of the eighteenth century, and admiring its little turned feet.

Arthur turned to notice a wash-stand – which, as Robin pointed out, are often misnamed 'wig-stands' – in three tiers connected by three wooden uprights. There would originally have been a washbasin in the top, a soap box in the middle, and a jug at the bottom. These have all gone, and it boasted instead a fine display of flowers (daffodils, jonquils and forsythia) making an exuberant display in the corner of the Hall. It was yet another example of an old piece of furniture given a new lease of life by its ingenious owners.

They came next to a piece not adapted for any other use – a bureau bookcase, made about 1715, in figured walnut, featuring candle-slides which in this example actually had candlesticks on them. These small candle-slides were made to slide back into the body of the piece of furniture when not in use. Arthur admired the piece as a whole, noting the quality of workmanship and the weight of the bureau flap, while Robin pointed out what excellent timbers were used, and noted the herringbone inlay, which matched on the bookcase above and the bureau below. This indicated that the bookcase and bureau were originally made for each other, instead of being put together at a later date, as often happened with pieces of this kind.

Arthur mentioned how rare it is to find candle-slides

of the wings. It was duly carried out by a builder called Richard Pace, who lived in Lechlade. He produced a trade card showing drawings of various houses he had renovated, including Kingstone Lisle, but no one knows who was the architect who designed it, though it is thought to have been either Cockerell or Basevi. The trade card shows that the intention had been to add an extra storey to the central block, and to make the wings longer, but for some reason this was not carried out. It was probably shortly after this alteration that a new garden front, entrance hall and staircase were built and, as we will discover, they were to be much admired by Robin Butler in particular.

But initially Arthur was pleased to see the use that Kingstone Lisle's present owners, Captain and Mrs Lonsdale, had made of some of the objects here. He began by looking at what he called the largest peat bucket he had ever seen, from Ireland. As Robin observed, even its handles, cast in brass, are handsome. But what especially pleased Arthur was that this object should not be put near the grate, where it would look incongruous today, but was

Above *One of the pole screens in the Hall, with its triangular base containing a wooden Egyptian figure*

Left *The Hall and flying staircase at Kingstone Lisle. The Hall's architecture looks classical, with its draped figures atop the columns; but it is suspected to be the work of a later amateur, possibly the owner of the house at the time, Edwin Martin Atkins. The superb flying staircase, criss-crossing from side to side, is an unusual and delightful feature*

Right *A collection of caddies admired by Arthur and Robin. In the centre the elongated octagonal example is in satinwood, with three walnut ovals; either side of it stand an excellent pair of oval caddies decorated with neoclassical motifs such as swags of flowers, medallions and shells*

that still have candlesticks on them, and gave Robin a candlestick to look at. Robin nearly dropped it. The reason? He was unprepared for its weight and solidity. It is silver, but made in heavy-gauge metal so it is very substantial. The hallmarks looked as clear as though they had been put there yesterday: there was the lion passant denoting sterling standard silver, the leopard's head signifying London assay, the London date letter for the year 1740 and the initials 'JW', the maker's mark of John White. Robin decided that instead of simply trusting the hallmarked date, he would check that the candlestick was made in the manner of its time. By blowing on the stem of the stick, he revealed a vertical seam running up it. As he explained, candlesticks of the period were made in three parts – two semi-cylindrical sections plus one for the lower part and base; these were then soldered together. This stick also features a late eighteenth-century crest depicting a phoenix, with a viscount's coronet above. It is a fine object – and all the more valuable for being one of a set of four, all of which are in the house.

Arthur then handed Robin a glass object that looked like a smaller version of a candlestick. One of Robin's areas of specialisation is glass, and he quickly identified it as a taper stick. It would have housed a small candle in the top and its function was to melt sealing wax for sealing letters. Sometimes they were made *en suite* with the candlesticks in the room; they can be found in brass or silver as well. Glass ones were intended to be used but had one major

practical disadvantage: as Robin put it, 'as soon as the candle burns down to the top of the glass stick – bang! That's it!' This example, which was quite early, had clearly been protected against danger.

Arthur then looked up and noticed another impressive glass object: an eight-light chandelier hanging from the ceiling. It features cascades of rosettes flowing down to hide the central column, and pear-shaped drops on the sconces. The way it sparkles, through the refraction of light through the glass, is quite spectacular.

Robin dated the chandelier as a fairly late example of its kind – probably about 1825; the date of the Hall itself. The architecture of the Hall appears classical, and includes draped figures standing on top of ornamental columns under a vaulted ceiling, but Robin was of the opinion that it is not quite as it should be. It is a very late interpretation of the style and executed with a sure-handed certainty, but he felt there were a number of features that were slightly wrong, indicating that it might be the work of a talented amateur.

Whoever designed it – and Arthur and Robin did not have time for a detailed examination – it is clear that he was highly ingenious. One end of the Hall is full of elaboration, as Robin pointed out, and the other is much more stark and simple – except for a remarkable flying staircase criss-crossing from one side of the Hall to the other. As he noted, it is a most unusual feature, with two separate flights spanning the gap and connecting the rooms on both sides. One or two flying staircases exist in other houses, but none is as extraordinary as this.

Meanwhile the Entrance Hall had further treasures to offer, and Arthur's eye was taken by two small fire screens or pole screens. He has seen thousands of such screens, many of which have not been too happily designed – but never a pair like this. Under the banner, in the open triangular frame, sits a wooden Egyptian figure. Robin suggested that it was inspired by the Battle of the Nile in 1798. Arthur added that at the time Nelson was such a hero that they made other furniture relating to him, such as rope-back chairs.

Close by on an adjacent side-table sat two oval tea-caddies. It is unusual to find a pair, as here, and these are of excellent quality. Arthur identified Robert Adam's favoured motifs, swags of bell flowers in inlaid satinwood, along with an oval satinwood medallion which has foliage growing up it in green-stained sycamore known as harewood. Robin was particularly impressed with the engraved decoration on top of the inlay which, as he noted, adds an extra quality to it. Arthur meanwhile was observing inlaid bands round the sides in kingwood, another favourite wood of Robert Adam's. On the top he identified a magnificent shell in satinwood with cross-banding in kingwood all the way round it. Robin thought the caddy weighed less than he would have expected, but when he opened it he saw the reason – it has an unusual laminated construction.

Arthur and Robin both thought these were superb pieces – as indeed was another caddy on the same table. This is a more usual elongated octagonal tea-caddy in satinwood. It features three ovals in walnut, and fine rope inlay around the edges. On the top is a stylish monogram.

From the Hall Arthur and Robin entered the Drawing Room where some fine furniture and other objects are housed, including two collections: glass, from the seventeenth and eighteenth centuries, collected by Captain Lonsdale; and miniature furniture. It was to a table upon which a selection of these small items was displayed that Arthur and Robin went first.

Arthur immediately picked up a pole screen, perfect in its miniature detail; next to it was a mahogany box with a door, like a cupboard. Nothing remarkable about that, you might think: but when he opened it what was inside it but a delightful chest of drawers, a few inches in height! It

has brass handles, two short and three long drawers, and dates from the late eighteenth or early nineteenth century. Like the box, it is made in mahogany. Arthur couldn't remember having seen a chest of drawers like it before, with its own box to keep it in. As he pointed out, objects such as these were a kind of catalogue. They would have been made by apprentices to a cabinet-maker, and sent out as samples to potential customers. Many are delightful little items. Robin next picked up a tripod table also in mahogany, constructed just like a full-size one, with a tip-up top – another charming and pretty piece.

Arthur was meanwhile admiring a miniature mahogany bureau from the early nineteenth century, complete with fittings beneath the flap, and long drawers underneath. Taking one of the drawers out, he discovered to his astonishment tiny copies of *The Times* and *The Tatler* inside. Clearly all kinds of miniatures have been collected here, so that they go together. The two tiny publications were much more recent, dated 1932 and 1930 respectively.

Lastly from this little collection Robin stopped to look at another tripod table, the top of which had a raised and moulded border like a piecrust – a copy, rather than an original, this time. He then turned round, only to spot a similar original, full-size one. And a selection of the fine glass from the cabinets had been taken out and put there on display.

The first piece Robin looked at was a small punchbowl – perhaps the right size for two people to take their punch

Left *Some of the miniature furniture examined by Arthur and Robin, including the pole screen, the chest of drawers, the bureau and the piecrust table*

Right *The Drawing Room at Kingstone Lisle. On a circular tripod table in the foreground stands a small glass punchbowl, a decanter and a pair of glass candlesticks, all of which Robin particularly liked*

from, but by no means big enough for a party. It features what is known as 'nipt diamond waies' decoration, which was applied in a manner similar to piping the icing on a cake. It was a method used as early as the late seventeenth century: glass threads were trailed onto a vessel, and then pincered together at intervals, to make a network of lozenges. Beneath the bowl is an inverted baluster, on a folded foot which, as Robin explained, has had the glass folded over the edge and tucked in underneath for reinforcement. The base is, to use his word, striated or ridged. Arthur mentioned that he always looks for what he refers to as the 'grain' on the base. Both noted that the way the punchbowl was finished led to its surface being not quite smooth. Nowadays steel tools are used, but wood was employed in earlier days – and Arthur judged that this piece dated from around 1690-1700. He pointed out that the punchbowl, like other pieces of glass on the table, had a lovely black colour, which was a sure guide to its age.

Robin turned next to a large goblet from around 1770. It has substantial wheel-cut decoration on the bowl, and the stem is faceted. This faceting – cut glass, in other words – was developed in England around the middle of the eighteenth century, and soon became very popular.

Next to the goblet was a pair of glass candlesticks, also with faceted columns, and of similar date. These were 'magnificent objects', in Robin's words, and like the silver candlesticks were very heavy indeed. He considered that they were probably Irish, partly because they didn't have the same tax on the weight of glass over there, and could therefore make it heavier. Arthur agreed as to their nationality but more because of the way the glass was cut, particularly on the base: it has a pared, rather than a deep, kind of cut. But Robin pointed out that it is very difficult to be certain where such pieces come from, or to ascribe them to any particular factory. Many people simply call such objects 'Waterford', but they are often wrong. There were also factories at Cork and elsewhere in Ireland. And Anglo-Irish cut glass was widely imitated in Europe and the USA right through the nineteenth century; particularly prominent were the Bohemian glasshouses, and those in Silesia.

Moving away from the table, Arthur came to a corner side-table upon which was a book-carrier – an excellent piece executed in rosewood, as was usual, and with beautifully turned spindles. This one has the bonus of a drawer underneath, and in it a piece of paper with the history of the book-carrier written down. Apparently it was first given by William IV, and then passed to various owners, all of whom are noted, right down to the present

Far left *The small punchbowl with 'nipt diamond waies' decoration. It was made around the end of the seventeenth century and its lovely black colour is a guide to its age*
Left *The 'nipt diamond waies' decoration shown in close-up: molten glass threads were laid over the bowl and pinched together to form a network of lozenge shapes*

Right *The two glass candlesticks with faceted columns, dating from the late eighteenth century. They are very heavy, and were probably made in Ireland*

Left *The splendid pair of candelabra dating from about 1840, on the mantelpiece when Arthur and Robin saw them, but photographed here on the Adam-style semicircular table on which the book-carrier was seen*

Right *The Jacobite carafe with its engraved emblem of a rose with two buds, signifying the Old Pretender and his two sons*

day. It is rare indeed to find a piece provenanced in this way – a family often knows the history of objects it owns, but seldom writes it down for future generations.

The table upon which the book-carrier sat was also an object of Arthur's interest. It is semicircular in the neoclassical style. As Arthur noted, Robert Adam designed pieces such as this and had them constructed by cabinet-makers such as John Linnell – he even had some of them made up by Chippendale! The cabinet-makers could show off their skills on this type of furniture, and here there is a feast of marquetry decoration, including a half-shell in the deep yellow of satinwood subtly contrasting with the lighter yellow of holly.

On the mantelpiece was a pair of candelabra – or 'two-branch table lights', as Arthur called them. Intended to stand on a big dining-table, they are quite magnificent. They date from around 1840, and the deep cutting on the faceted stem is crystal sharp; they also feature some

beautiful ormolu. All in all, Arthur was very taken with them.

Robin meanwhile was looking at what sits between the two table lights on the mantelpiece – an early basket-top bracket clock – and was finding it delightful. Under the number 'VI' are the words *Johannes Knibb Oxon fecit*. As Robin explained, though Thomas Tompion is known as the father of English clock-making, the Knibbs were also a fine family. Their clocks were noted for their very elegant dials: this one has simple cherub spandrels. A very fine, unusual clock, it dates from around 1680 and is an eight-day repeater with an alarm mechanism; when pulled out by Robin it struck 'one', then in a lower tone, 'one' again, signifying a quarter past one, which means the clock is a quarter repeater. It has 'IIII' rather than 'IV' on its dial and Robin explained that clocks often favoured 'IIII', to avoid any possible confusion of 'IV' with 'VI', which looks similar at a quick glance. When they did use

Sitting in the armchairs, Arthur and Robin were shielded from the fire by another pole screen. This gave Arthur the opportunity to describe a useful feature of pole screens: that the banner can be raised or lowered on the pole, so that when raised, for instance, it could shield the delicate facial complexion of a lady, but the fire would still warm her legs and ankles. Arthur and Robin had to conclude their visit here, though Arthur first exhorted anyone who came to visit not to ignore the other rooms in the house, nor indeed the gardens and façade.

One feature that will be noticed throughout, not least in the Drawing Room, is all the needlework. The carpets in this room are modern, of William Morris design, and were hand-made in gros- and petit-point. It took twelve girls two years to make each of the carpets. The last pole screen that Arthur mentioned has as a banner one of the many examples of the work of Mrs Lonsdale's mother.

Mrs Lonsdale herself contributed the tapestries on the chairs in the Morning Room and Hall. The Morning Room still boasts the original 1677 panelling in pine, though it has since had many coats of paint. Much of the furniture is of the Queen Anne period, and there are some fine paintings, including a picture of Whitehall by Wheatley, and other works by Constable, Paul Sandby, Monamy, Van Goyen and John Crome.

In the Dining Room the paintings are all of the family, apart from an overmantel painting of Kingstone Lisle Park by Lady Gascoigne. The window opposite the door was originally a door leading out to a formal garden, and the ceiling must have been put in much later. The furniture is made to designs by Sheraton, whereas in the octagonal Sitting Room there is Queen Anne period lacquer and another example of Mrs Lonsdale's work: a carpet specially designed for the room, which took seven years to make.

The other area open to the public is the Billiard Room, which comprises the whole of one of the wings added in 1820. All the windows facing the drive are dummies, which adds to the impression gained from outside that the house is much bigger than it actually is.

And though it may not be the largest or most spectacular house Arthur has visited, it is none the less unusual and fascinating. Arthur and Robin especially enjoyed that extraordinary flying staircase and the fine collection of glass.

'IV' it was a way of indicating that they used a method known as Roman striking, where two bells were struck, enabling the mechanism to go on for longer.

Arthur and Robin then sat down on a pair of Chippendale-period open-arm mahogany easy chairs of the type known as Gainsborough, to look at some glass displayed on another table before them. Robin noted first a set of four decanters, with faceted decoration – two of half-bottle size and two of full-bottle size – with spire stoppers, dating from around 1770. With them was a set of six wineglasses, also with faceted stems. But the *pièce de résistance* was a Jacobite decanter with engraved emblems of the Jacobite cause – on the back the motto *Fiat*, and also a huge engraved rose with two buds representing the Old Pretender and his two sons. But the vessel has a smooth neck – and in fact is not a decanter at all but a carafe, and a magnum at that, so that it holds two bottles-worth. A considerable rarity.

SHUGBOROUGH HALL

Arthur Negus's guest at Shugborough, the ancestral home of Lord Lichfield near Stafford, was David Howard, who had accompanied him a year earlier to Wilton House. Arthur had cause to remind David of their previous meeting right away, as they began their tour of the house at the fire-place in the Dining Room – a very similar fire-place to one in the Single Cube Room at Wilton where they had commenced that visit. The Dining Room boasts several very fine features apart from the fire-place, among which are some paintings of classical ruins and above the fire-place a portrait of the eighteenth-century Admiral George Anson.

George Anson provided the money for the remodelling and fitting out of Shugborough, the details of which we shall hear about later; but it was really his elder brother Thomas, as David explained, who was responsible for the way the house turned out. Though the tall central block of the house was built in 1693, and the estate – a riverside landscape which has changed somewhat in the last two centuries – was acquired by the family in 1624, it was during Thomas's ownership in the 1740s that Shugborough received its flanking pavilions and an interior transformation. And Thomas used George's money to good effect, going to the most prominent people in their fields for his purchases and commissions.

One example stood on the chimney-piece right by them: one of a pair of blue-john urns, which Arthur described as quite nice and simple. Matthew Boulton, regarded as the greatest English ormolu-maker of them all, was responsible for the excellent ormolu work on it.

Arthur then moved across to the dining-table to show David something he particularly liked – a Regency elbow

Left *The east front of Shugborough, dominated by Samuel Wyatt's portico of 1794. Either side of it are the pavilions built half a century earlier by Thomas Wright, with their semicircular bay windows and domes*

Right *One of the Regency carver chairs in the Dining Room, from a large set which probably originally comprised twenty-four chairs altogether. Its legs are what Arthur terms 'Trafalgar-shaped', and it displays the plentiful use of cast brass*

Left *The Dining Room. Part of Thomas Anson's additions to the house in about 1748, this room served as the Drawing Room until 1794. The ceiling features elaborate plasterwork by the Italian, Vassalli; Admiral Anson's brother-in-law thought it 'the best I ever saw'*

There might originally have been 300 or 400. That is not a particularly remarkable number, but what is special about the plates is their design, which was unique at the time. Arthur pointed out the armorials, and then noted the presence in the design of a coconut tree, a favourite dog, and even a Chinese version of a hollyhock. David identified other motifs such as the bread-fruit tree in the centre. Bread-fruits saved George Anson (then a Commodore) and his crew when they came ashore exhausted and almost starving after crossing the Pacific, and the plate also shows Plymouth Sound, with the Eddystone Lighthouse moved aside a bit to help the design, the anchorage at Wampon, and motifs such as flaming hearts, a quiver and love-birds – all sorts of thoughts of home. And in a volume of Anson's *Voyages*, which David found in the Library and which was published in 1748, there is an engraved illustration entitled 'A View of the Watering Place at Tenian' which has similar elements. But the design must have been given to the Chinese before the book came out, because Anson's arms on the plates are those of Commodore, not of Baron, which he became in 1746.

As Arthur commented, in those days you would put your armorial on just about everything, particularly on silver. It is unusual to find silver of the period that is not decorated with some symbol of ownership. So saying, he showed David one of a pair of silver salvers, with an armorial in the centre. It was made and assayed in London in 1747, and is the work of a silversmith described by Arthur as 'the Tompion of the silver world', Paul de Lamerie. He was a Huguenot who fled France, setting up in London and entering his first mark in February 1713. He became goldsmith to the king in 1716, and later produced some of the finest pieces of English rococo silver. Arthur showed David the almost three-dimensional quality of the decoration on the cast border, pointing out the incredibly realistic grapes, vines and tendrils. To have such a pair of salvers is remarkable indeed.

But David was equally fascinated by the armorial in the centre. The coronet over the arms was received by Anson when he became a baron and, as is the custom with baronial arms, there are two supporters – on the left a sea-horse, and on the right a sea-lion. The sea-lion is unusual in its naturalism. The Heralds would normally have decreed that it should have a lion as its top half, and a dolphin as its bottom half. But that would not do for

chair with what he liked to call 'Trafalgar-shaped' legs. Apparently these days no one uses that term, which reveals its date; 'scimitar-' or 'sabre-shaped' legs is now more widely used. This is a nice piece of early nineteenth-century work, involving the plentiful use of brass decoration, which came strongly back into fashion with the Regency styles. It features cast-brass acanthus leaves – as David noted, pinned on or appliqué. There is a cast-brass medallion in the centre of the back, and higher up gilt brass mouldings all round the top of the back and down it as well. Round the table Arthur counted eight singles and two elbow chairs. David suggested that this was a somewhat small set for such a large table. Arthur's answer was that there were probably more originally. One clue lies in the way chair-makers used to number their chairs, by marking one of the seat rails with Roman numerals using a ½-inch chisel. So you might see a couple of gashes on a chair, indicating that it is number two of the set. Arthur and David picked up a single, and saw the number XIIII carved into it; so it is the fourteenth chair of the set. There were probably as many as twenty-four originally.

If that sounds a lot, the plate David then picked up from the table is one of a service from which 205 pieces survive.

Anson, and looking again at the *Voyages* book, David turned up an engraving of a sea-lion drawn on Juan Fernandez, the first place they landed after rounding the Horn. One of the islands of this group was home to Alexander Selkirk for some years and is therefore the real setting for Defoe's *Robinson Crusoe*, which was based on his life. Arthur looked at the engraving and noticed that the sea-lion seems to be smiling – and its tail looks like a bunch of sprouts! And as David added, it's copied exactly onto the silver. No engraver would have known what a sea-lion looked like, unless he copied it from the book.

Arthur then asked David about Anson's voyage – was it purely one of discovery? It was not, in fact. The Lords of the Admiralty sent him to the Pacific to harry the Spaniards. We were at war with them, and his job was to sink or capture as many Spanish ships as possible and make life generally uncomfortable for them all the way up the Pacific South American coast. Anson's expedition seems to have been very successful, culminating in the extraordinary capture off the Philippines of the galleon *Cobadonga*, carrying an enormous treasure from Acapulco. When the crew returned, having circumnavigated the globe, they brought back with them £400,000 worth of gold and silver – that's between £18 million and £20 million today. As Commodore and captain, Anson would have received three-eighths of it as prize money, and this financed the work at Shugborough.

Arthur then picked up a silver-gilt punchbowl bearing an engraving of Anson's ship. As he said, he is often asked just what silver-gilt is. It is silver coated or plated with gold by a process similar to that used for ormolu. (See the chapter on Weston Park.) The punchbowl has some slight damage which conveniently demonstrates this: around the top is some embossed work of grapes and vines, but in one place some of the gold is missing, exposing the silver – so it is evident that the rest is gold plated on silver. The punchbowl was made in London in 1768, the eighth year of George III's reign, and the embossed work dates from that time. The engraving of the ship is also original – but there is some extra decoration around the bowl, in the form of foliage. Arthur reckoned that this was added in Victorian times, by people who thought that a lovely punchbowl like this, bearing a little beautiful engraving, was too plain. So they livened it up a bit – and both Arthur and David wished they hadn't.

The original engraving is excellent. It features the arms of both Anson, who died six years before the bowl was made, and his wife, and also a curious cartouche or frame around it, with soldiers, marines, a Chinaman, and even a box marked 'HY SON No.49' – a tea chest, presumably containing Anson's favourite blend of tea! There too is Anson's ship the *Centurion*. As David went on to explain, its story is quite bizarre. It set sail as part of a small squadron and was about as ill-equipped as it was possible to be. They had too few crew, and too few marines. The Admiralty ordered 259 Chelsea Pensioners to march from Chelsea to Portsmouth to be put aboard; not one of them survived the voyage. When Arthur said he was surprised they even made it to Portsmouth, David's reply was that two of them very nearly didn't – they were carried on to

Left *One of the plates from Admiral Anson's armorial service. The arms are those of Commodore, not of Baron, so the plates must have been ordered before he received the title in 1746. The design of the plates, featuring a number of unusual motifs, was unique at the time*

Right *One of a pair of silver salvers by Paul de Lamerie, dating from 1747. This time the armorial in the centre features the coronet that designates Admiral Anson a Baron. The crest's supporters, appropriate for a seaman, are a sea-horse and a sea-lion*

Right *The oval Sheraton period wine cooler, in mahogany and lead-lined on the inside. As you can see, it is in pristine condition*

Left *The silver-gilt punchbowl from the Dining Room, showing the engraving of Admiral Anson's ship, the* Centurion, *and the embossed grapes and vines round the rim*
Below *This detail from the punchbowl clearly shows where the gold that was plated onto the rim is missing, exposing the silver beneath. The engraved foliage below is probably a Victorian addition, and does nothing to enhance the decorative effect*

the ship on stretchers and died just after they set sail. With such an inauspicious start, it was remarkable that the voyage went on to be so successful.

A plainer object, seemingly untouched since it was made, was nestling underneath the table on which the salvers and punchbowl were displayed: a Sheraton period oval mahogany wine cooler, veneered with lovely 'flame curls', and of beautiful quality; it is lined on the inside with lead. Arthur often gets asked where people got their ice from in those days. He explained that it was usually stored in ice-houses in the grounds of houses like this. Somewhere in a fold of the earth there would have been an underground ice-house. When the ponds were frozen over, great chunks of ice would be cut and stored, and the earth's insulation was enough to keep the ice solid until needed. It would then have been transferred to a wine cooler lined with lead. But where did the water go when

representing the adventures of Dionysus with the Tyrrhenian pirates, whom he transformed into dolphins. Stuart had spent some years studying the buildings of Athens and participated in a revival of interest in Greek architecture. He also designed the other classical garden buildings.

The Triumphal Arch is a copy of a second-century AD arch erected by the Roman Emperor Hadrian to mark out the boundary of the city of Athens. It was transformed into a memorial for Lord George and Lady Elizabeth Anson. Peter Scheemakers carved the cenotaphs supporting busts of the Admiral and his wife flanking a central trophy symbolic of the spoils of war. The mason, John Hooper of Woodstock, estimated a price of £282.14s.1d. for the arch in 1761.

The Tower of the Winds is a reproduction of the Horlogium of Andronikos Cyrrhestes in Athens. The original tower has sculpted reliefs of the winds in the frieze, of which there is no trace in the copy. The ground floor was converted to a dairy for Lady Anson, while the upper floor with its beautiful panelled ceiling was reputedly used by the 1st Earl of Lichfield for gambling, when ladies ceased to be admitted to the tower. We shall hear more of his love of gambling, and where it took him.

There are several other follies as well, not all of which are copies of Greek originals, although the Doric Temple is almost identical to one at Hagley, Worcestershire, which is reckoned to be the first accurate version of a Grecian building in England. The Ruin, by contrast, was originally much bigger and included a Gothic pigeon tower. Tradition has it that it incorporates fragments from the former palace of the bishops of Lichfield. It features a seated figure reputed to be a Druid.

Two other follies might be linked to Anson's voyage: the Cat's Monument is said to commemorate the cat which travelled with the Admiral in the *Centurion*, although it could have been erected in memory of a Persian cat kept by Thomas Anson. The Chinese House, however, was definitely designed from a sketch by Piercy Brett, one of Anson's officers on board ship. It was completed in 1747, not long after their return from the circumnavigation of the globe, which had involved a prolonged stay in Canton. It is probably the earliest of the garden buildings.

the ice melted in the warmth of the house? Lifting the cooler from its stand, Arthur showed that in the centre of the underside is a small tap for drawing off the water into a receptacle placed beneath.

As David pointed out, there is an ice-house in the grounds near the Lanthorn of Demosthenes. This is one of the classical temples or follies that Thomas Anson had built, as part of his contribution to Shugborough. He was a keen classicist and, apart from the follies, amassed a famous collection of paintings, including those which hang in the Dining Room, depicting classical ruins.

Arthur and David went outside to look at these garden buildings. The Lanthorn of Demosthenes is also known as the Choragic Monument of Lysicrates, or more simply as the Dark Lantern. It was erected by James 'Athenian' Stuart as a copy of an original in Athens dating from the fourth century BC, which featured a sculpted frieze

As David mentioned, it is not unusual to find stone follies in lovely grounds such as those here, but it is even

more interesting when such views are brought inside, as it were – reproduced on pottery or porcelain. They had gone to the Blue Drawing Room and were looking at a piece of porcelain on a table – an exceptional item made by Josiah Wedgwood in around 1776, and one of only fifteen known pieces sent to Russia as samples for the famous 'Catherine the Great Service'. This one, a beautiful sauce tureen, features the Triumphal Arch in a painted scene with the title 'In Shugborough Park', along with three other pictures. All known samples feature English scenes and also a painted frog! So this is a very rare piece of porcelain, not least for its unusual shape.

The tureen was displayed on this occasion upon a splendid Regency games-table, which Arthur liked very much. It has lyre-shaped supports underneath, which are shapely and lively. The top is also fine, with green baize covering. The centre section has a sliding top, which is inlaid for chess and draughts; when you slide it back you

discover a leather lining marked out for backgammon. The table has semicircular ends, which open and would have contained chessmen, red and white draughts, dice throwers, dice – everything you would need for gambling.

This table was fortunate to survive the depredations caused by Admiral Anson's great-great-nephew, the 1st Lord Lichfield. As we have seen, he was a notorious gambler, and not one of the luckiest; he brought Shugborough to the brink of ruin. In 1842, as Arthur recounted, a sale was held at which just about everything was offered under the auctioneer's hammer to pay for Lichfield's debts. It was a tragedy that this had to occur, but certain items were not sold. Originally there were three games-tables: the first fetched a price of 10 shillings at the auction, and was taken away; the second went for a more modest 7s. 6d.; but nobody at all bid for the third one, so it stayed where it was – and getting on for a century and a half later, it came to be admired by Arthur

Left *The sauce tureen made by Josiah Wedgwood for the 'Catherine the Great Service'. The words 'In Shugborough Park' can just be made out below the painted scene, which features the Trimphal Arch in particular*

Right *The Regency games-table, which survived the enforced sale of 1842. It features lyre-shaped supports and has a green baize covering on the top, inlaid for chess and draughts. The semicircular ends would have contained chess pieces and the like*

Negus in the Blue Drawing Room. A very fine table – and a lucky escape.

Arthur was also impressed by the chairs near the table. They date from the Regency period, and, like the dining chairs before, feature Trafalgar-shaped legs and brass decoration. As he asked, has anyone ever seen better anthemia, or honeysuckle, than envelop the square panels in the backs of these pretty little music chairs? It is not unusual to find one in a house where someone in the orchestra played an instrument such as the harp or cello. But at Shugborough when they held a recital they took care to look after the audience, for there are no fewer than twenty-two of these chairs. The ladies and gentlemen would sit on them and listen to the music – but they were not made too comfortable, in case they fell asleep!

Arthur then spied some much larger gilt armchairs in the corner. He commented that you might think by looking at them that they are French. Certainly they were made to a French design – but in Lower Grosvenor Street, London, by one Charles Smith. A surviving account shows that he was commissioned to make fourteen armchairs and two sofas, for which he was to be paid the princely sum of £296. For this he also threw in 'shamey leather stockings' as he called them, to protect the front legs from clumsy housemaids. But what really appealed to Arthur was apparently a silk fringe, part of the upholstery, that ran all round the chair-seat and sides. In fact it is entirely made of carved wood. It fascinated Arthur that a man would go to all that trouble to create the permanent effect of a lovely silk fringe.

Above the armchair in question David looked up to see a Chinese mirror that also interested him. He pointed out the marvellous chinoiserie frame, and then went on to describe the mirror which has a reverse glass painting that dates from the time of Admiral Anson. Shugborough boasts a number of mirrors from this period, but David thought this one the finest with its picture of a warrior and his horse. The method of construction is worth mentioning. David explained that the decorators would order ordinary silvered mirrors from England. First they would clean off an area within the edge of the design they proposed to build up, so that only the sections not to be painted were left silvered. Then they would paint on the picture, such as this warrior – in reverse order. They would start with the pupils of the eyes, for instance, and

then fill in the whites around them; or the fine decoration and the gilding on the harness, then the harness itself, and then the horse behind that. Because it would eventually be viewed from the other side, through the glass, they started with the details and the foreground, and then painted on the background on top – otherwise it would have looked wrong when viewed from the front. David considered this one to be a superb example, from about 1750.

Arthur meanwhile also had a picture to show David – a framed page out of Chippendale's *Director. The Gentleman and Cabinet Maker's Director* was a book that came out in 1754; it contained a huge number of designs for furniture, which quickly caught on. The page that was framed displays a Chinese Chippendale break-front library book-case. And remarkably, right next to the chair and mirror stands virtually the same thing in real life – a huge library bookcase, with a superb pagoda on top, and pierced Chinese frets. Lower down, there is carving on the glass doors, and also the same motif carved below on the solid panel doors which would have housed big ledgers and large volumes. Arthur thought it remarkable to see something from near enough 1760 illustrated in this most important book of designs.

And there, sadly, the visit had to come to an end. As Arthur said, he and his companion never seem to get all that far round a house – but at least this time he and David managed to have a look at the grounds.

Shugborough goes back before Admiral Anson's time. Until the Reformation it belonged to the bishops of Lichfield. It was later acquired by a Staffordshire lawyer called William Anson. His grandson, another William Anson, demolished the existing house and in 1693 began to lay the foundations of a new one, the square three-storey block that forms the centre of the present building. His sons transformed the house and park. They were Thomas, who succeeded to Shugborough in 1720, and George, the admiral and baron about whom we have heard so much. Thomas Wright, an astronomer, mathematician and designer of Nuthall Temple in Nottinghamshire, was probably employed to undertake these alterations.

Wright constructed pavilions with domed bow windows that flank the existing house, but most of his other additions were remodelled or removed later on. Some rooms that he designed remain, including the Dining Room in which Arthur and David commenced their visit

Above *A Chinese mirror in the Blue Drawing Room. Dating from around 1850, it has a magnificent chinoiserie frame, and an excellent reverse glass painting of a warrior and his horse*

Left *One of the set of twenty-two music chairs, intended not simply for musicians to sit on while playing, but for an audience to sit on while listening to a recital. It features a delightful brass anthemion on the back*

Above *The framed page from Thomas Chippendale's* The Gentleman and Cabinet Maker's Director, *depicting a break-front library bookcase*

Right *And here it is in real life: a large Chinese Chippendale break-front library bookcase almost identical to the one in the* Director. *It has a splendid pagoda on top, and pierced Chinese frets, and dates from around 1760*

and the Library. In 1748 Lady Anson's sister-in-law wrote that 'the house has some fine rooms lately added to it, and one exceedingly odd and pretty that is the Library'. The room is in two parts, one in the central body of the house, the other in the link to the south pavilion, joined by a flattened arch cut through the old outer wall. The ceiling features rococo plasterwork decoration, believed to be the work of Vassalli, an Italian plasterer whose work can also be seen in the ceiling of the Dining Room. Sadly, the sale of 1842 accounted for almost all Thomas Anson's fine collection of books – including a number of rarities on archaeological and architectural subjects – so that the bookshelves now contain mostly nineteenth-century volumes.

When Thomas Anson's great-nephew inherited Shugborough in 1789 he called in Samuel Wyatt, one of the famous family of designers who reappear in other chapters of this book, to enlarge and remodel the house. He altered the links from the central block of the house to the pavilions, rearranged Wright's original balustrade, and added the portico to the entrance front. He also cased the entire exterior in slates painted to look like stone. Possibly this curious choice of materials is linked to the fact that Wyatt's youngest brother Benjamin was agent to Lord

Penrhyn, who owned almost all the slate mines in north Wales at the time. Later, most of these slates were removed and replaced with stucco.

Wyatt also rebuilt various interiors, the largest and most impressive of which is the Red Drawing Room. He joined together a bedroom and dressing room in Wright's north pavilion, and pushed the whole west wall further into the garden, to create a delightful room with a coved ceiling. The plasterwork here is by Joseph Rose the Younger (Robert Adam's favourite plasterer) in conjunction with Samuel Wyatt. It features a number of familiar motifs – anthemia, lyres, delicate wreaths and sprays of acanthus – in an elegant neoclassical design.

This room houses most of the armchairs and sofas in the set by Charles Smith, one of which Arthur examined in the Blue Drawing Room. Most of the other furniture was acquired by the 2nd Earl of Lichfield in the middle of the nineteenth century. After his father had caused so much to be removed from Shugborough in the 1842 sale, he set about collecting a good deal of excellent French furniture, and it is thanks to him that the house still contains so much of interest. A few remnants of the famous collection of paintings amassed by Thomas Anson hang in this room, but most were dispersed in the sale.

The Hall was remodelled by Wyatt to be a noble, classical setting for some of the best of the Greek and Roman sculptures collected by Thomas Anson. As with the books and paintings, a few remain, but most are gone. Though the room was part of the original seventeenth-century house, Wyatt gave it its present oval shape, introducing a number of scagliola columns with Doric capitals. The Saloon, the other major room altered by Wyatt – albeit ten years after his other alterations – also features Grecian columns. This time there are two rows of large yellow scagliola columns with Corinthian capitals. These are very accurate copies of the capitals used by James Stuart on the Temple of the Winds outside; perhaps they were even intended as a tribute by Wyatt to his distinguished predecessor.

So as well as its unusual set of temples and follies, Shugborough has some fascinating rooms and contents on show. Not the least interesting of these, as Arthur and David Howard discovered, are those associated with that pair of brothers, the admiral and the classicist, George and Thomas Anson.

DUDMASTON

Dudmaston is an estate that lies just to the south-east of Bridgnorth, in the county of Shropshire, and overflows with paintings, objects and books on one subject in particular: flowers. This was to be the theme of Arthur's visit, and so he invited as his guest a friend whom he knew would find it fascinating: George Smith, whose artistry in flower arranging is admired worldwide.

Two families have lived at Dudmaston since the house was built in 1697, but its origins go back even further. It seems there was a knight's dwelling here from the twelfth century, when one Helgot of Holgate granted a half hide of land to a Norman, Harlewyn de Butailles. There were also Tudor buildings here of which remains are left – but they give away little of their original structure or purpose.

So at the end of the seventeenth century Sir Thomas Wolryche commissioned a new house, which is the core of the present Dudmaston. He probably employed the architect Francis Smith to design it, though there is only circumstantial evidence to support this theory. In its entire 850-year history Dudmaston has never been up for sale, having always passed by descent or devise, but this does not mean its history has always been easy or smooth, and the present house has had a somewhat chequered career.

Thomas's son, Sir John Wolryche, seems to have been somewhat dissolute. His activities have been described as 'irresponsible extravagance', and his death 'early, but not exactly untimely'. John laid out vast sums on his hounds and horses and on cock-fighting. He died by drowning in the river Severn while returning home from celebrating a win at the Chelmarsh races in 1723. He seems to have lived hard and played hard, but he may not necessarily have worked hard: on his death Dudmaston faced his own debts, his father's debts and also settlements and jointures that almost ruined the estate. It passed eventually, after various owners, into the hands of William Whitmore, but by then its silver and furniture were mostly gone. Frances

Left *The east front of Dudmaston. Relatively little of the ground and first floors of this side have altered since the house was built in 1697, though the roof and attic storeys were transformed in the 1820s*

Whitmore, his daughter, later wrote this:

> My father found Dudmaston a large and in some parts unfinished house quite empty. I have heard him say he could find nothing when he took possession – but an old pair of yellow breeches. . . He said to his Housekeeper Mrs Harling – I suppose I shall want a few things in your line look about and get them – Want a few things in my line Sir, why you want but everything in every line.

It was William Whitmore's son, William Wolryche-Whitmore, who was responsible for major alterations in the 1820s, in between, that is, being a Whig MP, an advocate of Catholic emancipation and the repeal of the Corn Laws, and a pamphleteer on free trade, the railways, agricultural prospects and wine duties. During a visit to Italy in 1814 he even found time to visit Napoleon on Elba. At Dudmaston he hired a local builder to alter the roof-line and add pediments and a parapet; at this time the Library and Staircase Hall were also formed. It was in the Staircase Hall that Arthur and George Smith began their visit.

The stairs are a delight, skilfully cantilevered with delicate and precise neoclassical detailing. They have white walls and a green carpet. But at the foot on this occasion was something the visitor will unfortunately never see: a tall pedestal flower arrangement specially created by George. As Arthur stopped to admire it, George described it as a breath of spring. He found the staircase light and elegant and so chose pale lemon, cream and white flowers – forsythia, prunus blossom and very fragrant mahonia – with green echoing the carpet.

But there are other features here that are more permanent. Arthur showed George a Chinese *famille verte* vase dating from the K'ang Hsi period, 1662-1722, which stood on a commode. In the panels on the vase baskets laden with full flower arrangements are depicted in magnificent enamels. George was suitably impressed, particularly as the Chinese started the art of flower arranging. But their designs tended to be more sparse, so he suggested this one may have been made to appeal to western markets.

Arthur then took his guest over to a George II chair, dating from 1730 at the latest. The carving on it is of excellent quality, featuring two little tassels at the top of the rail, as if they were cords to draw what looks like a carved curtain. The cabriole legs are also covered in crisp carving, leading down to the ball and claw feet. No flowers? Only on the seat where a copy of some Georgian

needlework depicts what George identified as carnations, tulips and lilies. This needlepoint was in fact worked by the present occupier, Lady Labouchere, who was Dudmaston's owner until she gave it over to the National Trust in 1978. Her grandmother, Alice Mary Wolryche-Whitmore, was the daughter of Alfred Darby of Coalbrookdale whose wife was a Christy. These family connections resulted in a number of items making their way to Dudmaston, including Francis Darby's collection of flower paintings and Alexander Christy's furniture and collection of objects made of Derbyshire spar stone or blue-john. Lady Labouchere's husband, Sir George, has also made significant contributions to the house, including a fine collection of modern paintings and sculpture.

Arthur had meanwhile moved on to a long-case clock in

Above *The face of the Samuel Whitchurch clock with the dial showing high water at Bristol above, and morning glories engraved around the centre*
Right *The Staircase Hall, an airy and elegant area formed in the 1820s. The stairs are cleverly cantilevered, and feature delicate neoclassical detailing. The Hall has been refurnished since Arthur and George's visit*

Left *A detail of the Chinese famille verte vase from the K'ang Hsi period, 1662-1722, featuring enamelled panels showing baskets laden with flowers*

Left *The painting in the Staircase Hall of two Dutch girls holding tulips. The picture was probably executed for the express purpose of publicising the tulips, as Holland was undergoing an obsession with these flowers at the time*

Right *The Library. This room was created in the 1820s by amalgamating what had been two rooms, to form a library/living room of a kind fashionable at that time. The bookcases are modelled on those at Weston Park, and the room was painted white in 1967*

the Staircase Hall. He described it as a good, simple, mid-eighteenth-century example whose maker, Samuel Whitchurch, was known to be active in Bristol in 1765. It features a dial to show high water at Bristol, and another depicting the phases of the moon, scaled to twenty-nine and a half days, with an eight-day striking movement and a brass and silvered dial. Nothing extraordinary so far, but the brass is, very unusually, engraved with flowers. George noticed that these are morning glories which only last one day. They open in the morning, and are shut and finished in the evening – an ingenious and appropriate decoration for the face of a clock.

George then spotted a painting above a commode, depicting two Dutch girls in prim dresses, carrying tulips. He was impressed with the way the tulips were painted; as the purpose of the picture may well have been to publicise the tulips, this is perhaps not surprising. He was able to

date the painting to the first quarter of the seventeenth century, which was the time at which tulips were being bred on a huge scale in Holland. The tulip originated in Turkey and was first cultivated in the second half of the sixteenth century. Europe went mad over them, and the Dutch most of all tried to develop all manner of new varieties, particularly striped ones. Enormous amounts of money changed hands – and not only money. For one bulb the following goods were given: 2 loads of wheat; 4 loads of rye; 4 fat oxen; 8 fat pigs; 12 fat sheep; 2 hogsheads of wine; 4 barrels of 8-florin beer; 2 barrels of butter; 1,000 lb cheese; a complete bed; a silver beaker; and a suit of clothes! Total value 2,500 florins. A name arose for the tulip obsession: *tulpenwoede* or tulipomania. And this is the name the Labouchere family give to the painting. Not surprisingly, the craze couldn't last; about 1637 the bubble burst and many investors were ruined.

Near the painting George saw some engraved illustrations from *The Temple of Flora*, which was produced by Robert Thornton between 1799 and 1810. He commissioned the best artists in the country to illustrate flowers, and then had them engraved by masters of the craft. Despite the quality of the book, it lost a great deal of money. Thornton was reduced to holding a lottery of the plates to recoup what he could, and he died a poor man in 1837. George looked in particular at two engravings showing different kinds of striped tulips – the very flowers the Dutch worked so hard to develop, and which did some of them no more good than the book did Thornton.

From the Staircase Hall Arthur and George entered the Library, which Arthur dated to about 1820 – as he said, pure Regency in style. Like the Staircase Hall, the Library formed part of the alterations commissioned by William Wolryche-Whitmore. By combining the drawing room and the saloon of the original house, Whitmore created a library/living room, of the type made fashionable at the time by Henry Holland. Certainly, as Arthur remarked, you have only to look around to know you're in a room that's lived in. Again, the theme of flowers predominates; Arthur even spotted flower-heads in the cornices of the bookcases on the wall (these were modelled, incidentally,

Right *The flower painting over the Library fire-place, by Van Huysum. Like the other flower pictures in this room, it was originally bought by Francis Darby in the years following the Napoleonic Wars*

Left *A Louis XV escritoire, dating from 1750-60. This is a fine piece of French furniture, with a good deal of excellent inlay*

and auriculas, a type of primula. These pictures were painted for very rich merchants who wanted to show off their possessions – like tulips, and other new plants coming into Holland at the end of the seventeenth and the beginning of the eighteenth centuries. But while these were show-pieces, the artists included the odd reminder of mortality – a decomposing leaf, or a fly, or the symbol of the free spirit, a butterfly.

These flower pictures come from the family's connection with the Darbys, and were originally bought by Francis, eldest son of the third Abraham Darby, who built the famous Iron Bridge across the Severn in 1779. Francis had a love of flowers right from his youth, and used to draw wild flowers whenever he was able. His artistic interest may well be the reason that very high standards of ornamental ironwork came to be achieved by the company at Coalbrookdale, including the massive iron gates for the 1851 Great Exhibition. Francis had a good eye for judging pictures, too. As George remarked, he bought his collection of flower paintings in the years following the Napoleonic Wars. This was an intelligent move, as Van Huysum in particular was so sought after that he never went out of fashion. But Francis didn't only buy flower paintings, he thought 'Mr Constable a very talented young man', and bought two early pictures of Hampstead Heath.

Van Huysum has been described as 'the last of the great Dutch masters', and was active during the first half of the eighteenth century. He was one of the few major painters who became very famous in his own time and whose fame has survived from the time of his death until the present day. His patrons included the Kings of Poland and Prussia, the Elector of Saxony, Prince William of Hesse, the Dukes of Orleans and Mecklenburg and Sir Robert Walpole. After he had been dead thirty years Catherine the Great, wishing to buy some of his works, found that a pair of them were valued at £1,200, twice as much as a pair of famous Rembrandts. Nowadays a Van Huysum might expect to fetch a cool £100,000. Mind you, he was apparently a meticulous worker; despite the importance of his clients, he would, as George recounted, quite happily keep them waiting for up to a year. If he didn't find just the right rose to paint – well, the picture would simply have to wait.

Below the Van Huysum picture Arthur pointed out a pair of splendid *famille rose* porcelain birds, from China.

on those at Weston Park). The Library also houses some good English and French furniture. Arthur pointed out to George a fine Louis XV escritoire or writing-desk, dating from around 1750-60. He described it as typically French, with its big fall-down flap. It also features a delightful oval wood picture in the middle, with garlands of flowers and leaves around it. This inlaid panel, depicting a boy with a musical instrument, is made with tulipwood, kingwood and purplewood veneers; the panels below and the ends are also covered with inlay. As George noticed, the lower doors feature swags of fruit tied with ribbon.

George then moved on to the three flower paintings above and on either side of the mantelpiece, by the Dutch artists Van Huysum and Van Os. Looking first at the Van Huysum painting, George pointed to the grapes, which were gorgeously and lusciously rendered. Arthur commented that he could happily eat them – but what he was mostly admiring was the energy and richness of the painting. George identified morning glory at the bottom

They are a delightful shape, with brightly coloured plumage, and Arthur described them as bold, important-looking objects – which they are, and very rare. Their condition is pristine; he wondered if they had stood there untouched since the 1820s.

And in the centre of the room Arthur found a small rectangular Chippendale table, from around 1760. As he explained, Chippendale had a weakness for the oriental in his later years, and this is a good example: it has bamboo-patterned cluster-column legs, supports and cross-stretchers and a pierced open fret border. Known as a silver table, it was simply intended for displaying pretty objects.

On this occasion it held some plates from Lady Labouchere's Coalbrookdale service. Each has a single flower design in the centre. Not surprisingly, the plates greatly appealed to George. He picked up one with a *Primula auricula* design – the same flower as he had just identified on the Van Os painting on the wall. This was a flower brought over by the Huguenots, who called it 'bear's ear', because of its little leaf which is shaped like a bear's ear. Arthur told George that Samuel Gilbert of Quatt, near Dudmaston, grew these flowers and wrote about them in the seventeenth century. Many people with cottage gardens had them, and still have them – they're well-loved flowers.

Arthur picked up another plate, featuring a foxglove. When he turned it over, he was delighted to see that the flower was named on the base. As he explained, in catalogue terms this makes it a 'botanical' rather than a 'floral' pattern dessert service. The addition of the printed name means that the service is worth about three times as much! Arthur also noted the other information on the base – that in 1820 one John Rose won a gold medal for his porcelain. That makes the service contemporary with the room, both bespeaking the Regency age of elegance.

George had meanwhile picked up a cakestand and noticed that it even had flowers painted on the underside. Featured this time was a *Rosa mundi* – which as George explained is a variegated rose with stripes – an old rose, but one that is becoming popular again now.

Moving to another table, George saw displayed S. T. Edwards's *Book of Flowers*. Leafing through, he stopped at a page on which three auriculas were drawn. As he noted, they were coloured in bright pink, yellow and purple, a

daring combination that most people would fight shy of. George went on to mention that a whole wing of Dudmaston is devoted to botanical drawings; in fact Lady Labouchere has collected them since the 1950s. Arthur and George were not able to go and look at them on this visit, but a number are on view, and include various hand-coloured engravings by the same Sydenham Edwards. He was the principal artist for the *Botanical Magazine* during its first twenty-eight years and also drew 'Hyacinths' for Thornton's *Temple of Flora*.

Arthur moved on to two delightful little circular tables, from the Regency period. They may even have been made for this room, as they keep good company with the Chinese Chippendale silver table and, with their bamboo underframing, do not differ too greatly in style. They are

Right *One of the plates from Lady Labouchere's Coalbrookdale service, featuring the* Primula auricula *design, dating from about 1820, the same period as the Library*

Left *The painting to the right of the fire-place in the Library, by Jan Van Os. Van Os is widely regarded as second only to Van Huysum as a creator of opulent flower paintings*

rosewood, with satinwood banding incorporating floral motifs in both the border and the centre.

But the next piece of furniture Arthur saw drew his opinion that for him it was the best piece in the entire house. It is a big, bold Chippendale elbow chair – one of a set of two plus seven singles, and there were possibly ten or more originally. The one Arthur was looking at was big enough to take the wide clothes of the period and was richly carved, particularly along the beautifully shaped top rail. It was signed all over with large and small 'C' scrolls, but its best feature was the shape of the arms. 'The way they come out with great turned-out knobs, you could just sit in them and grab them.' There is carved acanthus along the arm, and going down the supports. All in all, in Arthur's words, a fantastic chair.

In a corner was another flower painting, on an easel.

George immediately identified it as a Van Os, and noted that these days we've lost a lot of the flowers they used to paint, though some are being reintroduced. A pineapple provides an exotic touch, and there is the amusing feature of a mouse nibbling at grapes. At the bottom right, a gamebird hangs down over the edge giving the impression of a still life. But it is full of energy and movement – all told, a fine rococo composition.

Jan Van Os was active in the latter half of the eighteenth century, and is widely regarded as second in Dutch flower painting only to Van Huysum, who preceded him by some fifty years. In many ways his work was derivative of Van Huysum's – but then, if someone has painted the ultimate in flower pictures, which was what Van Huysum was widely regarded as having done, how can any subsequent artist attempt the same subject without some degree of imitation? In fact Van Os is reckoned to be almost his elder's equal in quality of detail, but not in terms of composition, and Van Os often used less sombre colours, which might have been more in keeping with contemporary tastes. He used to send his work regularly for exhibition at the Society of Artists in London – hence much of his finest work can be found in England, some of it at Dudmaston.

Arthur then pointed to the eighteenth-century French commode at the far end of the room and invited George to look at the flower motifs there. The commode itself is smothered with inlaid flowers; on it sits a pair of tall blue-john columns, with trailing vines and berries in ormulu. There is also a pair of blue-john cassolettes – little vases that are also candlesticks – with some excellent chiselled ormolu by Matthew Boulton, depicting swags of laurel. Arthur asked George what he would do if asked to create a flower arrangement for the Library. He answered that it would be a challenge he'd enjoy – to try to capture the spirit of the exquisite flower paintings. Then a rich and magnificent flower arrangement was brought in, which George had already prepared for the room. It was a magical way to end the visit for it was an arrangement on the grand scale, in the style of those flower paintings, incorporating grapes and other fruits and a great number and variety of colourful and exuberant flowers – a joyful and spectacular creation.

Although Arthur and George went no further, there are seven other rooms that can be visited, four of which contain art collections. Dealing with those first, Gallery One contains much of Sir George Labouchere's fine collection of twentieth-century painting and sculpture. He chose to collect abstract art, which he saw as the most exciting trend in art since the Post-Impressionists, in the 1950s; he now has a number of works by some of the most famous and remarkable artists of this century. Sculptures by Barbara Hepworth, Henry Moore, Jean Arp, Lynn Chadwick and others can be found in this gallery and other rooms. There is an impressive number of modern paintings, including some by Ben Nicholson, Max Ernst, Kandinsky, Vasarely, Miró, Matisse, Modigliani and Augustus John.

Gallery Two houses twentieth-century Spanish pictures mostly reflecting the darker side of Spain's recent history. The third gallery, by total contrast, contains a collection of topographical watercolours built up by Lady Labouchere since the 1950s. Some of these, such as the Royal Tomb in Granada, views of Barcelona, the Council Chamber in Bruges and a Chinese landscape were bought as reminders of countries in which Sir George served as an ambassador. Others are more local, depicting Ludlow Castle and buildings in Bridgnorth and Shrewsbury. The fourth gallery, as mentioned earlier, houses another collection built up by Lady Labouchere – botanical art. Here are twenty-five prints and drawings dating from the eighteenth century to the present day – from a signed *Narcissus* by the German G. D. Ehret (who is described as the dominant influence on botanical art during the mid-eighteenth century) to *Flower Studies* by John Nash, an important English artist of the mid-twentieth century.

Of the other rooms that can be visited, the Dining Room is only open occasionally; none the less it boasts a good number of further Dutch flower pictures by major painters, including Van Os. There is also a late eighteenth-century fire-place surround in marble with blue-john plaques, which complement the blue-john urn and vase there. This fire-place surround was bought fairly recently, as was another one now found in the Oak Room. This latter room houses a number of portraits of members of the owners' family, along with other paintings and drawings, and a bronze by Barbara Hepworth. It features oak panelling from the early eighteenth century, and the room itself has changed little since that time. The same can be said of the Entrance Hall, the last room that remains to be mentioned, though the first the visitor sees. Here hang portraits of Dudmaston's early owners and their relatives, and also three paintings of members of the household staff, which were almost certainly intended originally for the servants' quarters. There is some late seventeenth-century furniture, some of which was made for the house, including an oak and elm refectory table with one end incised as a shovelboard, and a fine, recently acquired set of William and Mary chairs and settees, with the original needlework worked by Lady Nottingham and her daughters for their home at Burley-on-the-Hill.

It is, however, the theme of flowers that characterises Dudmaston above all else, with flower motifs in nearly all the furniture Arthur looked at, and the excellent Dutch flower paintings that delighted and inspired George Smith.

Above *Arthur's favourite feature
from his favourite piece of furniture:
the arm of the Chippendale elbow
chair, with turned-out knobs, and
carved acanthus all along it and down
the supports*
Right *A big Chippendale elbow
chair – a particular favourite of
Arthur's. It comes from a set of dining
chairs of which seven singles and two
carvers survive, but which would
probably have comprised ten or more
chairs originally*

STRATFIELD SAYE HOUSE

Stratfield Saye is a country house and park situated between Reading and Basingstoke. The house was built in 1630 by Sir William Pitt, Comptroller of the Household to James I. The structure of the house has remained essentially unchanged since then, although the interior has been altered at various times, most notably between 1730 and 1790 when Pitt's grandson, Baron Rivers, owned it. And though the original Caroline house had been red-brick, in the eighteenth century it was covered with stucco.

Such is the early history of Stratfield Saye, but it is not for this that the house is famous, nor was it the prime reason for Arthur's visit. He brought with him his old friend and broadcasting colleague, Hugh Scully. Hugh is a collector of political cartoons and has a particular interest in Arthur Wellesley, 1st Duke of Wellington. Stratfield Saye was Wellington's country home after his victory at Waterloo, and is full of fascinating memorabilia; thus the house is important and exciting to modern visitors predominantly for its connection with him.

The first thing Arthur and Hugh looked at was a painting of the Great Duke – not as a commanding general on the field of battle, nor as a powerful prime minister, but as a private man, a kindly-looking Victorian grandfather. It was painted in the last year of his life, in 1852; he was eighty-three when he died. In the picture he is with four of his five grandchildren, one of whom, Arthur, was to become 4th Duke in 1910. As Hugh commented, he in turn was grandfather to another Arthur, the 8th and present Duke. So the picture demonstrates a family continuity which is reflected in the house – for Stratfield Saye has been the home of all the dukes of Wellington.

Arthur Negus perceived this sense of continuity in

Left *The west front of Stratfield Saye. The central block of the house has changed little since 1630, but two outer wings were added in 1846. The bronze statue in the foreground depicts a horse struggling with a dragon; it is actually incomplete, and should include a mounted St George*

147

Left *The Library, and beyond it the Music Room with its grand piano. A favourite room of the Duke of Wellington, it was designed in about 1740. It seems not to have changed a great deal from the time he used it, as the picture opposite shows*

another way. He had noticed in the background of the painting certain features – a chair and a bookcase in particular – which are still in the Library today, where the picture was originally painted.

And when they entered the Library, there it all was, with the grand piano in the Music Room beyond, through a set of doors just as in the painting, with all the original library bookcases in fine condition. As Arthur asked, by any standards it is a beautiful room, but how did Wellington come to be here?

Hugh's explanation was fascinating. After Waterloo, the nation in gratitude voted Wellington £600,000, so that he could purchase a house suitable for a great national hero to live in – a place like Blenheim, say, which had been built by the Duke of Marlborough a century earlier in very similar circumstances. Eventually, in 1817, after considering a number of possibilities including Bramshill and Uppark, the duke purchased the Stratfield Saye estate, then about 5,000 acres in extent, for £263,000 from the 2nd Lord Rivers. It was his intention to pull down the entire house and build towards the north-east corner of the park a new home that would be a worthy rival to Blenheim – a palace of grandeur. Several architects submitted plans. Benjamin Deane Wyatt, eldest son of the James Wyatt of Wilton and Goodwood fame, designed a vast, spreading palace with a huge central dome. Sir John Soane's protégé,

C. H. Tatham, suggested a long, more restrained house with a larger dome, and C. R. Cockerell planned an enormous house with a huge Grecian portico.

But it was not to be. Even with the generous parliamentary grant, Wellington could not afford to build such a home. Besides, his wife Kitty had immediately fallen in love with the existing house, and continued in her affection for it. So he plumped for the comparatively modest building that was already there, and in fact lived in it for the rest of his life. He altered it in various ways to make it more convenient and comfortable and was quite happy with the results, though his friends weren't, deeming the house too small and poky for such a distinguished hero.

The Library was a favourite room of the duke's. Its design and decorations date from about 1740 and are in the style of William Kent; he may even have designed it himself. Arthur's eyes went up to the ceiling – magnificent with its octagonal bosses and vast amount of gilt – from which hung some splendid lamps. As he said, it is quite easy to miss what is on the ceiling, as people take in the furniture and other objects, keeping their eyes low. But these lamps are of great interest. They are absolutely original, pure Regency, four-branch brass oil-lamps with mask heads underneath; all in all, really lovely.

The walls are covered with pale bluish-green silk,

matching the finish of the upholstery on the seat furniture. When Arthur and Hugh sat down they discovered that the chairs were really quite hard. As Arthur explained, these were not easy chairs – for this was where a gentleman would sit and work. All his books, his maps, his papers, would have been around him here.

On the arm of the chair he was sitting in Arthur found a device that would help: a revolving book desk, which would swing on the arm of the chair, with a ratchet to alter the angle of the reading surface – a useful invention, considering how large some books were in those days. Hugh added that, regarding books, you could almost call this a French library, for in one area of the room many of the books are in French. Wellington was, as Hugh pointed out, a Francophile. What's more, after Waterloo he virtually ruled France for a while. The Library also contains several books from Napoleon's library, which were presented to the 1st Duke by Louis XVIII.

Something else you expect to find in a library, Arthur pointed out, is a centrepiece, usually a library table of some sort. And he showed Hugh a delightful round example with a quite beautiful top. It is covered with one huge sheet of amboyna veneer, surrounded and cross-banded with coromandel; around that it has a plain band of paler wood, known as bird's-eye maple because of its markings of small spots, which seem to suggest birds' eyes. Outside that again is another narrow band of coromandel. Hugh remarked that it is a very attractive wood, and asked where it came from. Arthur replied that it is found on the Coromandel coast of India. It is often mistaken for ebony that has a little sap because of the pronounced white streaks; in fact it is as hard as a brick and very difficult to work.

So the table has a very good top – but Arthur was impressed with it for other reasons too. Turning it over, he showed Hugh the frame onto which a table-top is screwed or fixed. You might expect such a frame to be cut in segments out of thick lumps of wood – but not this one: it's made on a bench the proper way, with three 1-inch strips of wood all tongued together. The result is a tremendously strong frame, so that the top will never be able to move. But the maker wasn't satisfied even yet. He added to the frame four mahogany brackets with turned ends stained to resemble ebony, pretty cross-stretchers, some acanthus decoration on the leg, then higher up a few

blossoms and more acanthus and finally a carved tulip. But when the table is right-ways up, little of it is visible. As Arthur pointed out, this is how good cabinet-makers used to construct furniture; they weren't concerned with the time, they just said, 'This is how it should be made, and I'll make it properly.'

Another thing one looks for in a library is a writing-table. The example here is double-sided, for use by two people if necessary. For this reason it is free-standing and not designed to stand against a wall. There are three deep drawers on either side. As it is a Regency piece Arthur looked for, and found, on the end standards a beautiful stylised honeysuckle, that most popular of Regency motifs.

On the table was an inkstand which Arthur also admired. It was hallmarked in London in 1817 – the very year the Duke of Wellington came to Stratfield Saye. And its maker was the famous London silversmith Paul Storr. He designed many of the vessels which were ordered by the royal family from the firm for which he worked, and he has been called England's leading Regency silversmith.

Left *The walls of the Library are covered with a pale silk, as is the upholstery on the seat furniture. This silk was renewed to the original design in 1963. The bookcases, and many of the books themselves, date from the duke's time*

Right *A section of the top of the circular library table. The amboyna veneer is surrounded and cross-banded with the darker coromandel; this in turn has a band of bird's-eye maple around it, outside which again is a thinner band of coromandel*
Below *When the table is turned over, the extent of the craftsmanship becomes evident. The wooden frame's three strips of wood tongued together can be clearly seen, as can the mahogany bracket stained darker to look like ebony, and the carved tulip decoration at the top of the leg*

Arthur then picked up a goose-quill, which he was delighted to see was original, just as cut; the inkpot to dip the quill in was original too. And there was also a pounce-pot, or sander. If you had written a letter and the ink was still wet, you would pour fine white sand onto it to dry the ink. Of course, you then had to get rid of the sand, which could make something of a mess!

Also on the inkstand were some tiny taper sticks. Each has its own extinguisher and candle sconce – but everything is in miniature. So, when the duke wanted to send a letter, he would fold it, light the taper, and heat the sealing-wax. Eventually a blob of melted wax would fall onto the wrapper, and the duke would then take his seal from his fob (Arthur, who was demonstrating this to Hugh, had the duke's own seal in his hand) and would seal the letter.

And still on the subject of sending letters, Arthur then produced something for those interested in philately – a penny black, the first stamp issued anywhere in the world: it came out on 6 May 1840. A collector would ideally like not only a penny black in good condition, but also an interesting postmark: here the stamp has both. The postmark reads, though not very clearly, 'Dec 1840', so this stamp was used in the first eight months of its existence. As Arthur commented, most philatelists would call that a beautiful cover. But this one has merits that would appeal to autograph collectors too, for the letter is written by the Duke of Wellington himself, signed with just a 'W', from 'S-S, Dec 29 1840'. He was a prolific letter-writer, according to Hugh, and had the reputation of replying to every letter he received by return of post – a discipline not many of us share! No wonder he abbreviated the name of the house to 'S-S'. As Arthur said – fancy having to write 'Stratfield Saye' in longhand at the top of fifty letters a day.

Arthur then picked up a strange pair of objects that looked like very large soup spoons, and asked Hugh what he thought they were. They are made of tin, and japanned – which means they are covered in an imitation of oriental lacquer. On a piece such as this a black asphaltum varnish would probably have been used; the imitation would never have been convincing. There was also a little binding on one side to stop you cutting your ear – and that's the clue. For the two objects are early hearing aids. Arthur put one to his ear, and Hugh asked if he could hear him any better. Arthur replied that he could, but only because Hugh was talking more loudly!

Hugh then explained that the duke had been rather hard of hearing towards the end of his long life. There is some evidence that he was mistreated by his local doctor, whose disastrous efforts seem to have made him totally deaf in one ear. But what is known for certain is that he loved inventions and had several other hearing aids, including one shaped like a walking stick.

As Hugh noted, this liking for inventions was turned to practical account in the house. Not only did he install the almost unheard-of comfort of blue-patterned china water closets in each of the nine guest bedrooms but he also introduced a central heating system, which may have been the first in England. When Queen Victoria came with the Prince Consort to stay for four days, at her own invitation, she noticed the difference from the much colder Windsor Castle, and chose to describe Stratfield Saye as 'convenient but rather over-heated'. Later in life, Wellington was admired and respected by the Queen, who had become a close friend, but when she was younger she had

been decidedly disenchanted with him, and even had to be pressured by her favourite, Lord Melbourne, into inviting him to her wedding in 1840. Whether or not this had anything to do with the fact that at her coronation the cheers for the duke had been louder than the cheers for the new queen, it is perhaps uncharitable to ask.

Hugh now began to leaf through a book containing political cartoons and caricatures pertaining to the Great Duke's life, and told Arthur about his long, occasionally stormy, career in politics. After Waterloo, to the considerable surprise of his friends, Wellington entered politics and took the post of Master General of the Ordnance in Lord Liverpool's cabinet in 1818. He spent twenty years in politics, three of them as prime minister, but it was not a wholly successful career. He had in fact always distrusted politics and politicians. In taking political office he made it clear that he would have nothing to do with party politics, but would do the job in question because he felt no one else could do it as well as he could, and because the good of the country came above every other consideration.

But these times were full of ferment, and Wellington found himself in the middle of a series of unpleasant occurrences. First, he took responsibility for the massacre at Peterloo, when in 1819 a crowd of 80,000 people met to discuss political reform. The local magistrate was worried enough to call in the cavalry, who proceeded to charge the unarmed mass – and there were 500 casualties as a result.

Then he found himself arbitrating in an unseemly royal controversy, after George IV succeeded in 1820. The new king had for years lived apart from his wife Caroline; should she be allowed to become queen? This undignified debate was eventually dragged through Parliament, but the matter was closed by her death in August 1820 (after she had been shut out from George's coronation in July). In 1828 the duke became prime minister almost against his own wishes and was faced by the Irish Question. He decided that the Catholics must be emancipated and brought this about against widespread vicious opposition. But he was not so keen on the Reform Bill, and his refusal to budge led not only to his eventual resignation as prime minister in 1830, but to his becoming a figure of public hatred. As one account puts it: 'He was hissed by mobs in London whenever he appeared; sackfuls of threatening letters arrived; a state visit by the king to the City of London had to be cancelled because of a real risk of

Right *The double-sided library writing-table. On the end standard it is possible to make out the anthemion motif, skilfully carved*

assassination. The duke took to carrying an umbrella ending in a sharp spike to protect himself from attack.' But finally Wellington realised that his stand against reform was futile, and in 1832 he let through the Lords the Bill which reformed the voting and constituency system and allowed for greater representation of ordinary people in Parliament.

Though he held parliamentary office again, he became more popular with the public as his political involvement decreased. He was still Leader of the House of Lords in 1842 when, at the age of seventy-three, he was asked to become Commander-in-Chief of the British Army, a post he had held more than once before. He retained this office, along with that of Warden of the Cinque Ports which he had accepted in 1828, until he died.

Having a life in politics on top of his military achievements, it is hardly surprising that he was the butt of cartoonists, and, as Hugh said, if you think today's cartoons are cruel, you should sample some of the nineteenth-century versions at Stratfield Saye.

The first one Hugh turned to depicts Wellington as a horse; the caption reads: 'TO BE SOLD with all his TRAPPINGS, that splendid charger ARTHUR, who served in the Peninsular and other campaigns, must be rode without a curb as he is not used to restraint, and will kick at it. He comes from a notorious stock, is thoroughbred, will not be warranted sound, must be taken with all his faults.'

It dates from 1820, shortly after the duke had entered politics. Another reflects the troubles the Tory party went through during this period. Entitled 'The Funeral of Tory Principle', it shows two lines of mourners, with Wellington in the foreground in one of the lines. And in yet another, this time even more cruel, he is depicted as a plague of vermin, chased by a dog and a farmer in a barn.

There is of course much more to see at Stratfield Saye, but Arthur and Hugh had no time to continue their tour. The present duke sums up the chief attraction of the house as an 'indefinable atmosphere', which makes it seem as if 'the Great Duke only left here twenty-five years ago'.

Left *The Paul Storr inkstand, dated 1817, complete with goose-quill, inkpot, pounce-pot, and even a taper stick to heat the sealing-wax*

Right *A letter from the Duke of Wellington. It carries a penny black stamp, and at the head of the letter it is just possible to make out 'S-S, Dec 29 1840', which was the first year of issue of the penny black*

Below *They may look like soup spoons that have had a chunk taken out of them – but they are really two of the Duke of Wellington's hearing aids, made of japanned tin*

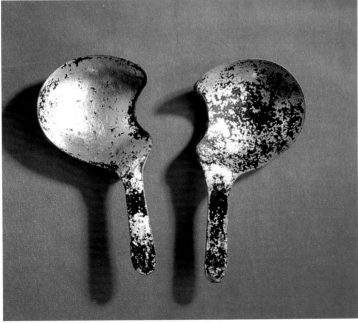

And though there are no great state rooms there is much worth visiting. The Hall, for instance, has a floor with Roman mosaics set into it. These were excavated by the 2nd Duke in 1866. The Gallery is supported by a number of Ionic columns which look like granite but are wood; and from the Gallery rail hang several banners. The biggest of them, in the centre, is the banner of the 7th Duke as Knight of the Garter. Around it are half a dozen smaller tricolours, embroidered in silver with imperial bees. These were originally presented by Napoleon to each department of France, and were given up to Wellington on his entry into Paris after Waterloo. There are two smaller tricolours at each end of the line of banners. These are presented every year by the duke to the reigning monarch, on or before Waterloo Day (18 June), and represent a kind of 'rent' for the house and estate. Some of the furniture here was bought by the Great Duke when the collection belonging to Napoleon's uncle was sold. The big tazza in green malachite near the fire-place is one of many examples of gifts received by Wellington from

LOT 1

TO BE SOLD with all his TRAPPINGS that splendid Charger "ARTHUR" who served in the Peninsular & other Campaigns – must be rode without a Curb as he is not used to restraint, & will kick at it – he comes from a notorious Stock & is thorough bred – will not be warranted sound, must be taken with all his faults & must be Sold

Left *The cartoon of Wellington as a horse, 'Lot 1' in a sale. The caption reads: 'TO BE SOLD with all his TRAPPINGS, that splendid charger ARTHUR, who served in the Peninsular and other campaigns, must be rode without a curb as he is not used to restraint, and will kick at it. He comes from a notorious stock, will not be warranted sound, must be taken with all his faults'*

European heads of state. It came from Tsar Alexander I.

There are a number of portraits on the upper walls, all of which depict dukes and duchesses of Wellington; on the lower wall are scenes from the Peninsular War. These campaigns were so named when in 1808 Wellesley, yet to become a duke, went as a lieutenant-general to the Spanish peninsula with 14,000 troops to assist the Spanish who had risen against Napoleon's brother, Joseph, imposed upon them as king. After Wellesley had won just one battle against the French, all the enemy troops were withdrawn. But in 1809 he had to go back again, because the French had returned to overrun Spain and Portugal. This time it took longer but in 1813 he cleared the French out of both countries and crossed into France. Six months later, Napoleon abdicated. He was sent to Elba; when he escaped, it fell to Wellesley, recently created Duke of Wellington, to sort him out again – which he did at Waterloo.

The Gallery houses a certain amount of French furniture bought by the 1st Duke in Paris in 1817, including some fine Louis XVI cabinets and commodes by Étienne Levasseur, in the style of Boulle. A series of bronze busts, some of them partly gilded, lines one wall. These represent various English and French monarchs and marshals, and two Roman emperors. The friezes which run along the top of the walls are taken from the Trajan and Antonine columns in Rome.

The Gallery has been restored to its white and gold eighteenth-century splendour and boasts prints on the walls, placed there by Lord Rivers, many of which show Shakespearian scenes. Clearly the duke followed the current fashion for attaching prints to walls, since he decorated other rooms in the same manner, including some bedrooms on the first floor and the appropriately named Print Room. Here the prints seem to fall into several categories or themes, and it is as if they were placed in position more to maintain the symmetry of the overall pattern than for any reason of subject matter. But Wellington did one thing in all the rooms he decorated in this manner: he always included one print of himself. Here, for example, there is such a print over each of the end doors.

The present family's principal sitting room is the Lady Charles Room. It takes its name from Augusta Sophia Pierrepont, who married the Great Duke's second son, Charles, and from whom all subsequent dukes have been descended. There are several paintings of her family on the wall, but above the door into the Print Room hangs a

Right *Wellington this time depicted in a caricature as a plague of vermin, chased by a dog and a farmer*

RATS IN THE BARN. OR JOHN BULLS FAMOUS OLD DOG BILLY ASTONISHING THE VARMENT

picture of a white horse – the first commission that Edwin Landseer ever received. He was sixteen at the time. It was painted in 1814 for Lady Charles's father – but disappeared before delivery. It was 1842 before it was discovered, in a loft over Landseer's stables, presumably hidden there by a dishonest groom. The artist, by then Sir Edwin, duly delivered it along with a bill for the fee he would have charged when he was an unknown youth – ten guineas.

The Drawing Room houses more eighteenth-century furniture, bought by the Great Duke in Paris in 1817, along with French wallpaper he put up in 1838. But the main feature of this room is the collection of paintings, which came into Wellington's possession in a somewhat unconventional way. On 21 June 1813, while Wellington was busy defeating Joseph Bonaparte in the Battle of Vittoria, the Frenchman decided to leave the field of play, along with his baggage train. The duke sent the cavalry after him, and recovered the carriage and baggage, but not Joseph himself. Among the booty was a large number of paintings from the Spanish royal collection, 'roughly rolled up with manuscripts, state papers, and even love letters'! They were sent back to England without a proper examination; some of the paintings were even used by Wellington's soldiers to keep the rain off their pack mules.

Once home, Wellington discovered just what he had and, though he offered to return them to Ferdinand VII, the Spanish king considered they were a just reward, and asked the duke to keep them. Most of these paintings, still in remarkable condition, are at Apsley House, Wellington's London home; the remainder are at Stratfield Saye.

There are other rooms worthy of mention but perhaps this tour should end with the Small Drawing Room, which also contains a number of paintings – though without such a dramatic tale to go with them. Apart from the picture of the duke as an old man which Arthur and Hugh had looked at first, there is a silhouette of the duke just before he went to Eton. It is the only existing record of him as a boy and was done in about 1780.

But, as young boy or old man, the 1st Duke of Wellington's presence is pervasive at Stratfield Saye: memorabilia are everywhere; paintings of him, his campaigns and his family abound; purchases by him and gifts to him remain; and even one of his original radiators, still working (though now connected to a somewhat more modern system), can be found in the Staircase Hall. Arthur and Hugh must have felt that they had visited Stratfield Saye not so much to see a house, as to call upon a great man.

INDEX

Page numbers in *italic* refer to illustrations

A

Adam, James, 37
Adam, Robert, 35-47, *38*, *39*, *46*, 57, 58, 76, 95, 114, 118
Adam, William, 37
agate ware, 89
Alexander I, Tsar, 156
Alexander III, Tsar, 103-4
Alexandra Feodorovna, Tsarina, 98, *98*
Alfred, King, 48
Altdorfer, Albrecht, 102
Andronikos Cyrrhestes, 127
Anson, Lady Elizabeth, 127
Anson, George, 121, 123-4, 127, 133
Anson, Thomas, 121, 127, 131, 132, 133
Anson, William, 131
Arp, Jean, 144
Atkins, Abraham, 109
Atkins, Edwin Martin, *110*
Aubrey, John, 55
Aubusson carpets, 18, 31-2
Audran, Michael, 76
Axminster carpets, 81

B

Bacon, John, 76, *78*
Basevi, George, 111
Battie, David, 61-9, 83-93
Beauvais tapestries, 106
bellarmine jugs, 10-11, *11*
Bermejo, 102
Binney, Marcus, 109
blackjacks, 12
Blenheim, 149
bodkins, 29
Boleyn, Anne, 8
Bonaparte, Joseph, 156, 157
book rests, 150
book-carriers, 116-17
bookcases, 131, *132*
Boulle, André-Charles, 57, 81
Boulton, Matthew, 40-3, *42*, 121, 144
Brett, Piercy, 127
Bridgeman, Lady Ann, 28
Bridgeman, Lady Elizabeth, 20, 22, *22*
Bridgeman, George, 31
Bridgeman, Henry, Baron Bradford, 20, 22, 31
Bridgeman, Mary, Countess of Bradford, 32
Bridgeman, Orlando, 31, 32
Bridgeman, Otto 28

Bridgeman, Selina, 31
Brown, Lancelot ('Capability'), 22, 93, 95
Buller family, 59
bureau, 77, 98-9, *99*
bureau cabinets, 59
Burney, Fanny, 88
Bute, John Stuart, 3rd Earl of, 95
Butler, Robin, 109-19

C

Canaletto, Antonio, 81
candelabra, 39, 118, *118*
candlestands, 85
candlesticks, 52, 88, 113, 116, *117*
caquetoire chairs, 13
card-tables, 17
Caroline, Queen, 152
carpets, 40
cartoons, 152, *156*, *157*
Catherine of Braganza, 45
Catherine the Great, 128, 141
Cesari, Giuseppe, 51
Chadwick, Lynn, 144
chairs, 64, 79, 87, 93, 121-3, 130, 136, 150; *see also types of chairs*
Chambers, Sir William, *73*, 76
chandeliers, 113
Charles I, King, 8, 45, 81
Charles II, King, 8-10, 45, 72
Charles X, King, 47
Charlotte, Queen, 18
Chatsworth House, 22
chests of drawers, 43, *46*
Chinese Chippendale, 64
Chinese porcelain, 11, 59, *68*, *69*, 136, *136*
Chinese wallpaper, 15, *16*, 17
Chippendale, Thomas, 43, *46*, 52, 57, 59, *63*, 85, 87, 88, 89, 91, 102, *103*, 118, 142, 143, 145
Cipriani, Giambattista, 40, 43
clocks, 39-40, *40*, 73, *74*, 79-81, 118, 136-8, *137*
cluster-column legs, 85, 87
Cockerell, C.R., 111, 149
Columba, G.B.I., 22
combs, 30
commode en tombeau, 66, 67
commodes, 62, 67, 144
Compton Place, 66
Constable, John, 119
Cowper family, 64
Coypel, Charles, 76
Cozette, Pierre François, 76
cream jugs, 18
Crome, John, 119
Cumberland, Duke of, 106

D

Daniel, Samuel, 55
Darby, Francis, 136, 141
Darcy, Lady Penelope, 62
Darcy, Thomas, Lord, 83-5
Darnley, Lord, 85
Darrel, William ('Wild'), 12, 19
Dasson, Henri, 93
de Calston family, 12
De Caux, Isaac, 51
de Clermont, Andien, *56*, 57
De Condé, Prince, 79
de Lamerie, Paul 123, *125*
de Lisle, Alice, 109
De Torby, Countess, 99, 103, 105
decanters, 119
Delanois, L., 79, *80*, 81
delft ware, 11
desks, 52, 66, *86*, 87, 88, 89, *140*, 141
Disraeli, Benjamin, 31-2
Dodin, Charles Nicholas, 66, 69
dressing-stools, 43, *44*
Du Barry, Madame, 79
Dudmaston, 135-45
Dutch cabinet-making, 29

E

Edward VI, King, 45, 54
Edward VII, King, 71, 81
Ehret, G. D., 144
Elizabeth I, Queen, 11, 18, 46, 54, 85
enamelware, 30-1
Ernst, Max, 144
escritoire, *140*, 141

F

Fabergé, Carl, 95, 96-8, *98*, 99, 103-6, *104*, *105*, *107*
Falbe, Madame de, 102
Fawkes, Guy, 46
Ferdinand VII, King, 157
Fernandez, Juan, 124
Fetherstonhaugh, Lady Meade, 40
Feurstein, Joseph, 81
finger stocks, 13
fire-places, 39, 40-3, *42*, 48, 76
Firle Place, 61-9
flower motifs, 135-44
follies, 127
footman's chairs, 57, 59

G

Gage, Sir John, 61-2
Gage, Joseph, Count of Spain, 65

Gage, Thomas, 1st Viscount, 64, 66
Gage, General Thomas, 65
Gage, Sir William, 64, 66
Gage, William Hall, 2nd Viscount, 64-5
Gainsborough chairs, 119
games-tables, 10, 128-30, *129*
Gascoigne, Lady, 119
George I, King, 90-1
George II, King, 91, 106
George III, King, 65
George VI, King, 152
Gibbons, Grinling, 87
Gilbert, Samuel, 142
Gilbert, W. S., 71
Ginsburg, Madeleine, 20-32
girandoles, 91, *91*
glassware, 114-16
globe bureau, 98-9, *99*
globe-stands, 111
Gloucester, Duke of, 16
Gobelins tapestries, 76, *76*
goblets, 116, *116*
Goodwood House, 71-81
Gordon, 5th Duke of, 81
Gordon, Hannah, 35-47
Graham, George, 73
Grenfell, Imogen, 64
Gunpowder Plot, 46
Gwynne, Nell, 45

H
Halifax, Edward Wood, Lord, 83
Hals, Frans, 106
Hamilton, William Gerard, 87-8
hearing aids, 152, *155*
Henrietta Maria, Queen, 81
Henry VIII, King, 8, 46, 51, 54, 61, 85
Hepworth, Barbara, 144
Highmeadow, 64-5
Holbein, Hans, 51, 55
Holland, Henry, 139
Hooper, John, 127
Hope, Charles, 37
Hopetoun House, 37
Howard, Catherine, 46
Howard, David, 48-59, 121-33
Hungerford, Lady Ann, 12, 19
Hungerford, Sir Walter, 12
Huysmans, Jacob, 45
Hyde family, 109

I
Imari porcelain, *68*, 69
Ingram, Arthur, 85

inkstands, 150-1, *154*
inlay chairs, 13
Irwin, Lady, *89*, 90
Irwin, Henry, 7th Viscount, *89*, 90

J
James I, King, 46, 85, 147
Jensen, Gerrit, 57
John, Augustus, 144
Johnson, Thomas, 85
Johnson of Chichester, 81
Jones, Inigo, 48-51, 59
Jonson, Ben, 55

K
Kandinsky, Wassily, 144
Kedleston Hall, 22, 35, 37
Kent, William, 53, *54*, 57, 91, 149
Kingstone Lisle, 108-19
Kneller, Sir Geoffrey, 79, 81

L
Labouchere, Sir George, 136, 144
Labouchere, Lady Rachel, 136, 142, 144
Landseer, Edwin, 156-7
leather flagons, 11-12, *12*
Leeds pottery, *87*, 89
Leigh, John Shaw, 102
Lely, Sir Peter, 45, 81
Lennox, Earl of, 85
Levasseur, Etienne, 156
library steps, 43, *44*
library tables, 150, *151*
Lichfield, 1st Earl of, 127, 128
Lichfield, 2nd Earl of, 133
Linnell, John, 118
Lippi, Filippino, 102
Littlecote, 8-19
Lock, Matthias, 91
Lonsdale, Captain, 111, 114
Lonsdale, Mrs, 111, 114, 119
Louis XV, King, 65, 69, 76
Louis XVIII, King, 150
Ludlow, Lady, 96, 106
Luton Hoo, 95-107

M
mahogany, 13
mantelpieces, *84*, 85-7
March, Lady, 73
Marlborough, Duke of, 149
Mary, Queen of Scots, 85
Mary I, Queen, 54
Massinger, Philip, 55

Matisse, Henri, 144
Melbourne, 1st Lord, 69
Melbourne Service, *67*, 69
Memlinc, Hans, 102
Mercier, Philip, *89*, 90
Meynell-Ingram, Mrs, 93
Michael of Russia, Grand Duke, 99, 105
miniature furniture, 114, *114*
Miró, Joán, 144
mirrors, 22, *23*, 26, 66, 91, 130-1, *131*
Modigliani, Amedeo, 144
Monamy, 119
Monk, General George, 8
Monteith, Earl of, 52
Monteroli, 47
Moore, Henry, 144
Moore, Thomas, 40
Morgan and Saunders, 98
Morris, Arthur, 66
Morris, John, 66
Morris, William, 119

N
Napoleon, Emperor, 150, 155, 156
Nash, John, 144
Nelson, Lord Horatio, 114
Newport, Lady Ann, 26
Newport, Lady Mary, 26-8
Newport, Sir Richard, 28
Nicholas I, Tsar, 99
Nicholas II, Tsar, 98, *98*, 104
Nicholson, Ben, 144
Northumberland, Dukes of, 47
Northumberland, Henry Percy, 9th Earl of, 46, 72
Northumberland, Sir Hugh Smithson, Earl of, 35, 43, 46
Nostell Priory, 22
Nottingham, Lady, 144

O
occasional tables, 77, *79*
Oeben, Jean-François, 100, *101*
ormolu, 26, 43, 62, 67, 85, *92*, 93, 121, 144

P
Pace, Richard, 111
Paine, James, 22
Panshanger Cabinets, 63-4, *63*
paperweights, 18
Parr, Ann, 54
Parr, Catherine, 54
Pascall, James, 91, 93
patchboxes, 30, 31

Pembroke, George Augustus, 11th Earl of, 52, 58-9
Pembroke, Henry Herbert, 2nd Earl of, 55
Pembroke, Philip Herbert, 4th Earl of, 51, 55
Pembroke, Sidney Herbert, 14th Earl of, 57
Pembroke, Thomas Herbert, 8th Earl of, 54
Pembroke, William Herbert, 1st Earl of, 51, 54
Pembroke tables, 16
Penrhyn, Lord, 133
Pepys, Samuel, 45
Pergolesi, Michelangelo, 47
Perritt, Thomas, 90
Petworth Park, 71
Pierce, Edward, 53
Pierrepont, Augusta Sophia, 156
pincushions, 29
Pitt, Sir William, 147
pole screens, 114, *114*, 119
Pomfret, Earl of, 87
Pompadour, Madame de, 81
Popham, Alexander, 8-10
Popham, Sir John, 12, 13, 18, 19
portraits, 20-2, *22*, 43-5, *53*, 55, 65, *72*, 74, *74*, 79, 81, 90-1
Portsmouth, Duchess of, 45
posset pots, 11
pot-pourri vases, 15
Price, Bernard, 71-81
punchbowls, 114-16, *116*, 124, *126*
Pushkin, Alexander, 99

Q
Quér"oualle, Louise de, 72

R
Ramsay, Allan, 65
Régence commodes, 66, 67
Rembrandt, 106, 141
Richmond, 1st Duke of, 72, 81
Richmond, 2nd Duke of, 72-3, 75, 81
Richmond, 3rd Duke of, 71, 74, 76, 81
Richmond, 6th Duke of, 71
Riley, John, 32
Rivers, 2nd Lord, 149
Rivers, Baron, 147
Roentgen, Abraham, 77
Roope, Richard, 13
Rose, John, 142
Rose, Joseph, 90
Rose, Joseph the Younger, 133
Rothschild family, 100

S
St Clere, Eleanor, 61
salt glaze, 11
salvers, 123-4, *125*
Samson, Emile, 55, 57
Sandby, Paul, 119
Sandon, Henry, 8-19
scagliola, 37
Scheemakers, Peter, 127
Schofield, John, 52
Scott, Sir Walter, 19
Scully, Hugh, 147-57
Sèvres porcelain, 47, 61, 63, 64, 66-8, *66*, *67*, 76, 81
Selkirk, Alexander, 124
settees, 57, 102, *102-3*
Seymour, Jane, 8
Shakespeare, William, 55
Shelton, John, 73
Sheraton, Thomas, 18
Shugborough Hall, 120-33
side-tables, 116-117
Sidney, Mary, 55
Sidney, Sir Philip, 55
Slaugham Place, 93
Smirke, Sir Robert, 95, 96
Smith, Charles, 130, 133
Smith, Francis, 135
Smith, George, 135
Smith, Michael, 79
Soane, Sir John, 149
Somerset, Duke of, 45
Spenser, Edmund, 55
Spitalfields silk, 40, *41*
spotted fruit painter, 16
Stanislaus II, King, 79
Stanley, Henry Morton, 71
Stanmer, 66
Storr, Paul, 150
Stratfield Saye, 146-57
Stuart, James 'Athenian', 127, 133
Stubbs, George, *74*, 75, *75*
Sullivan, Sir Arthur, 71
Syon House, 35-47

T
tables, 52; *see also individual types of table*
Temple Newsam, 82-93
Thornton, Robert, 139
toilet service, 22-6, *24-5*, *26*
Tompion, Thomas, 118
Toulouse, John, 16
turnery chairs, 12, 13, *14*

V
Van der Heyden, Jan, 106
Van der Velde, Willem the younger, 106
Van Dyck, Sir Anthony, 53, 55, 81
Van Goyen, Jan, 119
Van Huysum, Jan, 141, *142*, 143
Van Os, Jan, 141, *141*, 142, 143-4
Vandercruse, Roger, 77, *78*
Vasarely, Victor, 144
Victoria, Queen, 106, 152
Vile, William, 51, 52, 55, 74
Vulliamy, 39-40, *40*

W
wall-sconces, 26, *27*
wallpaper, 15, *16*, 17
Walpole, Horace, 87
wardrobes, 28-9, *28-9*
wash-stands, 111
Waterfield, Hermione, 95-106
Webb, John, 51, 59
Wedgwood, Josiah, *31*, 128, *128*
Wellington, 1st Duke of, 147-57
Wernher, Sir Harold, 99, 106
Wernher, Sir Julius, 96, 102, 106
Wernher, Lady Zia, 99, 102-3, 106
Weston Park, 20-32
Wheatley, Francis, 119
Whitchurch, Samuel, 138
White, John, 113
Whitmore, William, 135-6
Whitmore, William Wolryche, 136, 139
Wilbraham, Lady, 26
Wilbraham, Sir Thomas, 26
William III, King, 18
William IV, King, 116
Wills, Lady, 18
Wills, Sir Ernest, 13
Wilton carpets, 54
Wilton House, 48-59
wine coolers, 111, 126-7, *127*
Wolryche, Sir John, 135
Wolryche, Sir Thomas, 135
Wootton, John, 72, 75
Worcester porcelain, 15-18, *17*, *18*, *19*, 31, 64
Wright, Thomas, 131
writing-tables, 150, *153*
Wyatt, Benjamin, 132, 149
Wyatt, James, 58-9, 76, 79, 90, 149
Wyatt, Samuel, *121*, 132-3
Wycke, Thomas, 15

Z
Zuccarelli, Francesco, 47